D0296457

WITHDRAWN FROM
THE LIBRARY
UNIVERSITY OF
WINCHESTER

A MOVEMENT PERSPECTIVE OF RUDOLF LABAN

A MOVEMENT PERSPECTIVE OF RUDOLF LABAN

S. Thornton

Senior Lecturer, Laban Art of Movement Studio

MACDONALD & EVANS LTD
8 John Street, London W.C.1.
1971

First published May 1971

S.B.N.: 7121 1350 9

PRINTED BY Unwin Brothers Limited
THE GRESHAM PRESS OLD WOKING SURREY ENGLAND

Produced by letterpress 9819

Preface

The growth of "movement education" in Britain, indicated by the increasing use of this term, is due to the spread of the work and theories of Rudolf Laban. Before 1938, in Britain, little was known of Laban's studies in the field of human movement, yet it was his theories which led to so much controversy and change within physical education. Dance/movement education is not the logical development of the 1933 Syllabus but the result of the political situation in Germany in the late 1930s. If Laban like so many of his contemporaries had gone to America, physical education in England might not have undergone the sort of transformation it has experienced since the Second World War.

Laban's theories first made their impact through dance. The dance form he had developed, involving self-discovery, self-awareness, expression and communication, was seen by teachers of physical education to have such educational possibilities. When some teachers tried to apply these same criteria to nearly every branch of the subject, however, a split occurred in the profession. Over the past few years there has been a gradual acceptance of dance and physical education as different kinds of activity, and each is now able to develop in its own way.

The work and ideas of Laban have aroused considerable controversy and the desire to elucidate these theories and the principles upon which they were based supplied the impetus for this present work. Up to the present time Laban's philosophic writings have been scattered throughout many books and journals and it is the author's intention to bring together the philosophy of Rudolf Laban, the principles which stem from this philosophy and the movement principles implicit in Laban's own publications. Inevitably such an investigation leads to considerations of his life, the spread of his ideas and their effect on others.

Although the author's main consideration is the application of Laban's theories in education, it must be borne in mind that the phenomenon of human movement is a vast and complicated study. Laban's own research ranged over the whole spectrum of human activity and what is now termed "movement study" in education is generally an abstraction of Laban's perspective of movement. It is hoped that a work which clearly indicates both the scope and the opportunities inherent in movement study and which states, simply, the theories of Rudolf Laban will be helpful to those who teach movement and also make a contribution to any subsequent developments of Laban's work.

March 1971 S.T.

Acknowledgments

The original manuscript for this present work was submitted in connection with the Course of Advanced Study organised at the University of Leeds Institute of Education in association with Carnegie College of Physical Education. I am grateful to those who have answered my questionnaires, written to me, granted me interviews or loaned me material from their personal archives. I am indebted to Dr. M. G. Mason, who was my tutor at that time, for his constant interest and advice.

I was privileged to have the library facilities of the Art of Movement Centre placed at my disposal by Miss Lisa Ullmann, who also gave me permission to quote from articles written by Laban or herself as well as much encouragement and personal help.

I am grateful to the following authors and publishers for permission to quote from their books: G. Bell & Sons, Limited, for the extracts from *Physical Education in England since 1800* by P. C. McIntosh, *Basic Movement* by M. Randall and *Modern Ideas on Physical Education* by M. W. Randall; Adam and Charles Black for extracts from *Modern Dance, the Jooss–Leeder Method* by Jane Winearls; Basil Blackwell for extracts from *School Gymnastics* by W. McD. Cameron and P. Pleasance; Gerald Duckworth & Company Limited for extracts from *Posture and Gesture* by Warren Lamb; Her Majesty's Stationery Office for the extracts from *Syllabus for Physical Training for Schools* (1933), *Moving and Growing* and *Planning the Programme;* the Inner London Education Authority for the extracts from *Educational Gymnastics* and *Syllabus of Physical Training for Boys in Secondary Schools*; Macdonald & Evans for the extracts from *Creative Dance for Boys* by J. Carroll and P. Lofthouse, *Effort* by R. Laban and F. C. Lawrence, *Modern Educational Dance*, *Mastery of Movement on the Stage*, *Principles of Dance and Movement Notation* and *Choreutics* all by R. Laban, *Teaching Gymnastics* by E. Mauldon and J. Layson, *Games Teaching* by E. Mauldon and H. B. Redfern, *A Handbook for Modern Educational Dance* by V. Preston, *Introducing Laban Art of Movement* by B. Redfern, *Modern Dance in Education*, *Creative Dance in the Primary School* and *Creative Dance in the Secondary School* by J. Russell; Pergamon Press Limited for extracts from *Dance and Dance Drama in Education* by V. Bruce; Theatre Art Books for extracts from *Labanotation* by Ann Hutchinson; University of London Press Limited for an extract from *A Book of Physical Education Tables* by F. J. Marshall and E. Major; Ruth Morison for extracts from *Educational Gymnastics* and *Educational Gymnastics for Secondary Schools*; Marion North for extracts from *A Simple Guide to Movement Teaching* and *Composing Movement Sequences*; Diana Jordan for extracts from *The Dance as Education.*

I would also like to express my thanks to *The Guardian* for allowing me to quote from an article on the Keep Fit Association; the Laban Art of Movement Guild and the Physical Education Association for the extracts I have quoted from their respective magazines and the Schools Broadcasting Council for the use of statistical material.

I am especially grateful to my wife for her hours of typing and proof reading. The many and long discussions which began from her questions have contributed in no small measure to the clarity of the original and this present text.

Contents

List of Illustrations

Introduction

A great variety of different kinds of activity use and make reference to movement. To the musician it has one meaning, to the painter it implies something else, whilst to the teacher of dance or physical education it has yet other and distinct connotations. Underlying all these differences is a fundamental unity, for the word "movement" implies that something is happening. Movement is a universal human characteristic and a person's movement experience begins even before birth. Thus to study movement is to study man, for movement is both the medium and the vehicle for all kinds of human activity and a deeper understanding and a heightened awareness of movement can bring a greater richness to life.

Since the Second World War the work of one man, Rudolf Laban, has been very closely associated with the way in which movement can be used as a means of understanding man. His movement theories are based upon years of observing, recording and analysing human movement used during work and leisure activities. Laban's approach to movement was based on the discovery that there were common elements to all movement and in the late 1940s his movement analysis, enumerating these factors, was nothing short of revolutionary. This analysis and his movement notation, which he used in his own extensive movement investigations, helped Laban to discover links between previously unrelated aspects of movement and comprehend that movement was not simply a physical event.

Even before Laban arrived at his perspective of movement many of man's actions were recognised as conveying attitudes of mind or inner responses. Laban's work has increased the range of movement which is now given this recognition and, because of his analysis, a more accurate interpretation of such movement is now possible. Laban's theories thus provide a way of more fully understanding man, for they are aimed at stimulating an awareness and an appreciation of the reciprocal link between the body and mind as it is displayed through movement.

Laban's theories embrace both aspects of the body–mind relationship, for he maintained that movement which was stimulated by inner attitude carried responses which were often beyond words. He believed in the accuracy of such responses and maintained that movement is a diagnostic tool for the understanding of covert activity. He believed that expressive dance arose from this same inner agitation and that dance is a creative medium in which everyone can participate. Man uses movement to express himself; at the same time his movement can influence his inner attitude. In much remedial work it is accepted that systematic movement experience can help a person towards a more accurate understanding of himself and, by heightening his awareness of the non-verbal communication of others, assist him towards the formation of more meaningful relationships. When movement is viewed in this way it becomes a central feature of man's life since it is the medium through which inner attitudes are displayed and by which experience is enlarged.

Chapter 1

Biography of Rudolf Laban

Varaljai vereknyei esliget falyi Laban Rezso Keresztelo Szent Janos Attila, better known as Rudolf Laban, was born on the 15th of December 1879 in Bratislava, which was then part of the Austro-Hungarian Empire. His father, an officer in the army, hoped that his son would follow a similar career, and Laban did attend a military school but, after only a short stay, he decided that his real interest was art and at the age of twenty-one he went to study in Paris.

He tells us that in 1894, as a youth of fifteen, whilst walking in the mountains he was moved by a particularly beautiful sunrise and felt the urge to convey what he felt to others. "But how? In words, in music, in paint? But it was all too rich for that . . . I *moved.* I moved for sheer joy in all this beauty and order; for I saw order in it all. I saw something which is absolutely right, something which had to be so. And I thought, there is only one way I can express all this. When my body and soul move together they create a rhythm of movement; and so I danced."[1] This was the starting point of his study of people's movement, not only their dancing but their work and their acting, in order to increase his own knowledge and capacity to communicate; thereafter to pass on this experience to others once he had achieved this in himself. He was given an ideal opportunity to implement this study, for he always accompanied his father to whichever place his father was posted. Thus he was able to study not only the cultures of the countries bordering Czechoslovakia but also those in the Near East and North Africa. This study provided a basis for his future work.

He studied in Paris from 1900 to 1907 and pursued various courses of study at the École de Beaux Arts. During this time he showed special interest in stage design, drama and dancing, theatre architecture, décor and costumes. He appeared with a troupe in Montmartre, at the Moulin Rouge, under the stage name of "Attila de Varalja"; the money he earned probably helped him to pursue his studies. A design for a "Saltarium" won him a gold medal, but the design was far ahead of the building techniques of the time and, although twenty years later an attempt was made to erect his "Saltarium" at a Chicago World Fair, this was not possible as the technical difficulties were too great. He also began his first experiments with the dance script which later became known as "kinetography." There is a thread running through all these apparently unrelated activities, an interest in the "action" type of artistic activity. Laban was not drawn to an art form which relied on solitude and required solitary endeavour; he was committed to an art which needed active participation from more than one person. His deep-seated interest in people, their life and their movement seems to have dictated the courses of study he undertook and the activities in which he participated.

In 1910 he founded what, for want of a better term, he called a "dance farm," at Lago Maggiore, at which the whole community, after work, produced dances based on their occupational experiences. The "dance farm" idea sprang from Laban's desire to lead people back to a life in which art grew from their experiences. In order to do this they had to be brought out of the towns, for, in Laban's opinion, the "aim of man was his festive existence, not in the way of gluttony and uselessness, but as a means of developing his personality, as a chance to lift him into those spheres of life which distinguish man from animal."[2] Through this experience of the "dance farm" he realised more and more that his "dramas, songs and movement-scenes, in spite of the occasional use of the spoken word, did not belong to drama or opera but to the world of dance."[3]

For the three years immediately prior to the First World War, Laban, as well as directing the Lago Maggiore summer festivals at Ascona in Switzerland, directed the movement experience at a self-sustaining art colony there. At these festivals spectators were admitted but they usually ended up by joining in. Perhaps these festivals contributed towards the idea of a dance form which was natural for all people, which subsequently led to the "movement choir." He was seeking a dance drama which did not use the formal techniques of mime and classical ballet. By this time he seems to have formulated his method of training dancers but his philosophy of dance was still, as yet, unformulated.[4] It was here also that he began his studies of space patterns and harmonies.

The outbreak of the First World War stopped work on the building of an open-air theatre that Laban had begun. He went to live in Zürich from 1915 to 1918, abandoning the festivals at Ascona and Munich. He began to work on his dance notation and on "choreology," which he termed research into the art of movement. More and more his research stressed the nature and rhythms of space harmonies. During this time he established his own dance school in Zürich, where he staged several productions.

After the war *Die Welt des Tänzers* (*The Dancer's World*) was published by Walter Seifert of Stuttgart. Laban was called to the National Theatre in Mannheim to re-establish ballet and movement by the presentation of his own productions.[5] It was in Hamburg in 1922 that Laban first produced *Swinging Cathedral*, which "became one of our greatest successes with public and press."[6] By 1923 Laban had established dance schools in Basle, Stuttgart, Hamburg, Prague, Budapest, Zagreb, Rome, Vienna and Paris. Each of these was named after Laban and was directed by a former Laban master pupil. The work of these schools, directly responsible for "the rediscovery of dance as a means of education and therapeutic treatment in our time, originated undoubtedly from the aesthetic pleasure experienced by some teachers, doctors and industrial welfare workers when watching performances of modern stage dance. They came to us, the modern dancers, at first sparsely, one by one, but later in increasing numbers, to ask 'Couldn't you do this kind of thing with our children, our patients, our workmen?' So we did it, and with quite unexpected results."[7] Each Laban school had a "movement choir," as an integral part of the school. In places where there was no Laban school he established movement choirs. The term "movement choir" was coined during this period, but in fact the principle had been established before the war, at Ascona. Spectators who had witnessed a performance of his work had been inspired to do something themselves and so they had asked Laban to lead them in dance for their own pleasure. This was called a "layman's dance group" but it was a movement choir in all but name.[8] In such a "choir" the dancers are divided into three main groups in the following way: those having crisp erectness and elevation are called *high* dancers, those having a swinging heaviness are called *middle* dancers, those with an impulsive heaviness are called *deep* dancers. Laban himself was a *deep* dancer, as were Mary Wigman and Kurt Jooss, two of his most eminent pupils.[9] His dance works ranged from compositions for small groups (*Kammer Tanz*) to compositions for huge movement choirs, and from recreative dancing for the untrained to works for trained dancers in theatres. During this time he produced *Faust* and *Prometheus*, using a speech choir.

In 1926 Laban's Choreographic Institute, which until then had been in Würzburg, was moved to Berlin. He also founded a union for dancers, who at that time had no protection of this sort. The foundation of a centre where standards could be set and where educational and artistic matters could be discussed was a direct outcome of the union. At this time he became concerned with questions of copyright for dancers. He published *Des Kindes Gymnastik und Tanz* (*The Child's Gymnastics and Dance*) and *Gymnastik und Tanz fuer Erwachsene* (*Gymnastics and Dance for Adults*) by Stalling of Oldenburg. At the end of the year he visited America and Mexico and lectured in New York, Chicago and Los Angeles. It was during this visit that he met and influenced Irma Otte-Betz, who was the pioneer of American interest in the complex subject of notation and its further development.

The first Dancers' Congress was held in Magdeburg in 1927 and for this occasion Laban produced *Titan*. Towards the end of the following year Laban's book *Schrifttanz*,[10] presenting his recently formulated system of movement notation, was published. The object of this publication was to enable a dance to be reconstructed exactly from the written form. This method of notation received public acclaim at the Dancers' Congress at Essen and, soon after, the Society for Script Dance was formed. This society produced a magazine *Schrifttanz*[11] for about four years.

In 1929 Laban directed a huge pageant involving 10,000 performers, 2,500 of whom were dancers, for the Crafts and Guilds of Vienna. Also during this year he directed a movement choir of five hundred for the Mannheim Festival. These two festivals gave him the opportunity to "go into factories and workshops and study their basic movements."[12] This opportunity was not wasted, for it contributed greatly to his "interest in the improvement of working movement and the psychological attitudes of industrial man."[13] As a result of this he began a type of movement consultancy, which was put on a professional basis only when he joined Lawrence at the beginning of the Second World War. Also during 1929 Laban, at the request of the director, transferred his Choreographic Institute from Berlin to the dance department of the *Volkwangschule* in Essen. This was a municipal centre for a professional training in the arts and where the training in art, dance, drama and music was of a very high standard. This school already had two of Laban's former pupils on the staff: Kurt Jooss, as the director; and Sigurd Leeder, as the principal movement teacher. They were soon to be joined, at the invitation of Jooss, by Lisa Ullmann, so it is not surprising that the *Volkwangschule* developed into the Laban Central School. This year also saw Laban's first experiments with the making of soundtracks for dance films.

In 1930 he moved to Berlin to become director of the Allied State Theatres, a position he held for the next four years.

It was during 1932 that the work of Laban came to Great Britain. Lesley Burrows had just returned to England after completing her training at the Mary Wigman school in Dresden and had established a dance studio in Chelsea.[14] Joan Goodrich, about to take up an appointment at Bedford College of Physical Education, had been given permission to undertake an extra year's course in dance at the expense of the college and she decided to spend the year at the Lesley Burrows Studio. She spent two months, at the end of that year, at the Mary Wigman School, where the work "centred around the development of the body as an instrument of expression. Exploration of the possibilities was infinite—with no limitations. Beyond that the main headings for training were tension, relaxation, swing, spring, impact and impulse. Dance composition and movement observation were included, but the analysis was not along the lines introduced by Laban into England."[15] It is of interest to note that Mary Wigman, one of Laban's eminent pupils, was, even at this time, developing her own movement analysis. Diana Jordan, after expressing an interest in the work of Laban, was recommended by Joan Goodrich to attend the Lesley

Burrows Studio. Before embarking on the three years' training, Diana Jordan went to the Mary Wigman School during the summer of 1935. The value of the work in Dresden was, in her opinion, of enough value to encourage her to embark on training from 1936 to 1938 under Lesley Burrows. During this period of training Miss Burrows was joined by Louise Solberg, an American, who had trained under Laban.

In 1935 *Ein Leben fuer den Tanz* (*A Life for the Dance*) was published by Carl Reissner Verlag of Dresden. Laban's effective work in Germany was brought to an end in 1936. He had been responsible for all the movement which had been staged in connection with the Olympic Games and had choreographed an open-air production for one thousand performers in Berlin. He had notated the parts for this production and sent them to the participants, who formed sixty different movement choirs drawn from thirty European towns and cities. At the dress rehearsal 20,000 guests were present including representatives of the Nazi government who did not share in the enthusiastic reception. "The performance never took place because it was prohibited and so were all my other activities."[16] Laban's work was declared *staatsfeindlich*, "against the State,"[17] being regarded as not sufficiently nationalistic and too universal to be acceptable to the Nazi party. His work was banned throughout Germany and he was banished to the Schloss Banz in Staffelberg.

Laban spent the winter of 1937 in Staffelberg resting and recuperating. During his stay the village schoolmaster experimented with Laban's ideas on movement with his class. Laban was very interested in the method this master used to teach the children to draw. Laban felt that the children's drawings helped him towards understanding "the unknown state of the subconscious, released into conscious form through the mind of an uninfluenced child."[18] (It is typical of Laban that no further mention is made of this in any autobiographical notes to which I have had access.) In the discussions that ensued about the "different forms taken by living phenomena"[19] Laban made use of the crystal forms, which were used in conjunction with his spatial theories.

He emigrated to Paris, where illness caused him to be inactive, but he did lecture at the Sorbonne and at the International Congress on Aesthetics.

During 1934 and 1935 Lisa Ullmann and Kurt Jooss had arrived in England. Jooss had gone to Dartington Hall in 1934 whilst Lisa Ullmann had, in 1935, established at Plymouth the first movement choir in the country, under the auspices of the Workers' Educational Association. Laban arrived in England on the 8th of January 1938 and went to the Jooss–Leeder Dance School at Dartington Hall. Here he recuperated and lectured on the art of movement and the history of dance. His research at this time centred on the psychological effects of movement.

When the area around Plymouth became a defence area shortly after the outbreak of the Second World War and the prospect of invasion seemed imminent, Laban and Miss Ullmann moved to London. Here, in July 1940, Laban held his first movement course for teachers at the invitation of Burrows, Jordan and Solberg. This was the first of the "Modern Dance Holiday Courses" which were held until 1961 at such places as Moreton Hall School, Chichester Training College, Dartington, Ashridge and the Chelsea College of Physical Education.[20] When the bombing in London became severe Laban and Miss Ullmann moved to North Wales, near Aberystwyth. Here Miss Griffith-Davies asked Miss Ullmann to take movement courses for teachers in mid-Wales as well as students attending the University College of Aberystwyth and Chelsea College of Physical Education, which had been evacuated to Borth, near Aberystwyth.

In April 1941, Miss Ullmann and Laban were invited by the Ling Physical Education Association to give a lecture demonstration at a conference held at St. Margaret's School, Bushey, in Hertfordshire. For this conference it was decided that the demonstration would not be entitled "Central European Dance" but "Modern Dance." By 1942 it was felt that "Modern Dance" was no longer adequate as a title. After considerable discussion it was decided that "Modern Educational Dance" was more apposite since this indicated the emphasis as well as the field in which this dance form was appropriate.

It was also during this same year, 1942, that Laban was asked to investigate the possibliity of applying movement notation to industrial processes. The recording of industrial rhythms had, until then, been accomplished by filming the process, but this was no longer possible because of the shortage of film. The need to find some method by which women could be trained to do jobs previously done by men made it imperative to find another way of recording movement. Kinetography was just such a method and F. C. Lawrence, a prominent Manchester industrialist and now vice-president of the Laban Art of Movement Guild, because of the urgency of the situation, sent his niece to study notation. Laban's invitations to Manchester were so frequent that he decided to move there and thus began his association with Lawrence. Their book on *Effort*, published in 1947, was one outcome of their liaison. Until 1953 Laban continued to work in Manchester, applying his theories and analysis of movement, in terms of effort, to various fields.

In 1946 Lisa Ullmann, who had been his close associate since pre-war days, opened her Art of Movement Studio in Manchester. This became the centre for educational dance in England. The curriculum was based on Laban's space harmonies and his theories of the exploration of expressive movement through effort patterns. Laban lectured at the Studio, at Leeds University and at the theatre school of the Bradford Civic Playhouse, as well as producing plays in Bradford in association with Esme Church.

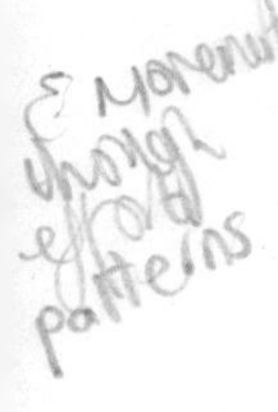

Two years after the foundation of the Art of Movement Studio, Laban published *Modern Educational Dance*,[21] perhaps the most widely read and therefore the most significant of his books. In the following year, 1949, the first Ministry-aided course in modern educational dance, having eleven students, began at the Art of Movement Studio in Manchester. In 1950 Laban published *The Mastery of Movement on the Stage*.[22] Three years later Laban moved to Addlestone, Surrey, where there were facilities large enough not only for him to carry on his own work and archives, but also to house the Art of Movement Studio. In an attempt to perpetuate his work, it was thought to form an organisation through which his work might become more widely known and to provide a centre for all those using Laban's principles of movement. In 1954, the Laban Art of Movement Centre was founded as an educational trust and it was during this year that *Principles of Dance and Movement Notation* was published.

Laban devoted the later years of his life to research

into various aspects of movement and to lecturing at the Studio.

Eight years after Laban's death, *Choreutics*, annotated and edited by Lisa Ullmann, was published. To date, this is the last published work attributable to Rudolf Laban, who died on 1st July 1958.

REFERENCES

1. *Laban Art of Movement Guild Magazine*, March 1956, p. 9.
2. *Ibid.*, October 1955, p. 16.
3. *Ibid.*, p. 17.
4. *Ibid.*, December 1954, p. 7.
5. Laban's dance dramas were as follows:
   1912, *The Earth*,
   1922, *Swinging Cathedral*,
   1925, *Don Juan*,
   1925, *The Fool's Mirror* (*Der Narrenspiegel*),
   1927, *Titan*.
6. *Laban Art of Movement Guild Magazine*, October 1955, p. 19.
7. *Ibid.*, May 1959, p. 20.
8. *Ibid.*, March 1956, p. 25.
9. Bodmer, Interview, *see* Appendix II, p. 122.
10. It is uncertain whether the title of this book is *Schrifttanz* or *Kinetographie Laban.*
11. *Schrifttanz*, published by Universal Editions, Vienna.
12. *Laban Art of Movement Guild Magazine*, December 1954, p. 41.
13. *Ibid.*, March 1955, p. 8.
14. Jordan, Interview, *see* Appendix II, p. 129.
15. Goodrich, Letter, *see* Appendix II, p. 130.
16. *Laban Art of Movement Guild Magazine*, March 1955, p. 9.
17. Bodmer, Interview, Appendix II, p. 122.
18. *Laban Art of Movement Guild Magazine*, December 1954, p. 22.
19. *Ibid.*, p. 22.
20. *Ibid.*, p. 33.
21. A new edition, revised by Lisa Ullmann, appeared in 1963.
22. A revised edition, entitled *Mastery of Movement*, appeared in 1960.

Chapter 2

Laban the Man

What sort of man was Laban? He could paint and draw, and could teach others to do the same. He designed buildings, recorded human movement in symbols and evolved a method of dance script which could be studied by all. His interests were wide and varied. He apparently studied human anatomy and physiology to a fairly high standard; he was familiar with crystallography and ancient Chinese contemplative exercises, religion in ancient Egypt and eighteenth-century mannerisms. Running through these wide ranging and at first sight unconnected fields of study, there is a common theme—the understanding of man. Man is the focal point of all Rudolf Laban's work and it is necessary to study his adaptation to the ever changing environment created by the course of civilisation. Man has to be observed in all his moods and in all those situations where human relationships are important. It is true that Laban studied movement, but he used this as a means to the study of man. For, to Laban, man is movement and movement is life.

It is important to consider how Laban appeared to those who met him briefly as a teacher, worked with him as a colleague or knew him as a friend. It is recognised that the following appreciation of "Laban the man" will be, to those who knew him, little more than a thumb-nail sketch. It seems necessary, however, to include the following details so that the people who never met him can begin to have some appreciation of Laban as a person.

As previously indicated, if there is one aspect of Laban which emerges more strongly than any other it is his understanding of people. He mixed easily with "his associates and students"[1] and he seems to have understood to an extraordinary degree the limitations and capacities of the people who were around him, no matter how brief the acquaintance happened to be. He saw people with startling clarity and this could be a most discomfiting experience. Laban did not attempt to change people, but accepted them as they were and encouraged them to develop their potentialities. He did not attempt to make them "fit a pre-cast mould."[2] By using his understanding of people he helped them to "move on, to search and find their own solutions."[3]

> "Laban could see the detailed and also the thing as a whole. And he was interested in both and particularly in relationships, how one aspect affected or modified another. Because he made his students aware of the basic truths about movement, the subsequent developments and application of his teachings have not followed the same paths as with a teacher who provides set exercises or ideas. Exploration, investigation, finding out for oneself were part of his training. Not all are capable of taking advantage of this freedom, and many students yearned for material to be dumped in their laps ready made. But this was not his way, and he discouraged in his educational work any establishment of set patterns."[4]

Laban wanted each person "to reach the greatest self-understanding of which the individual was capable and was prepared to drive them if he thought that would help"[5] but he would never drive an individual unless this was necessary and it would never be done for Laban's personal satisfaction but only to make it possible for a person to "discover certain things within herself."[6] His method, if such a word can be used, of helping a person towards understanding himself was always tailored to the needs and capacities of the person concerned.

Laban could draw out of people, through his understanding of them, abilities which they never dreamed they possessed. He was able to do this because he could "see something good in what everyone did,"[7] and therefore could find the strengths of that particular person, exploit those strengths and expect the individual to do the same. Laban was able to do this because of "his patience in illustrating or explaining just what he wanted to teach. He had the ability to make each person feel that he was the most important being in the class and that his difficulties and capabilities were of paramount importance. He gave his undivided attention to each pupil and he had the ability to fill each person with a burning enthusiasm for learning and perfecting what he had learnt."[8] This ability of Laban's to see something worth while in every task a person had to fulfil meant that constructive criticism, and therefore encouragement, was the fundamental precept of his teaching.

Therefore, after a session with Laban "you left him encouraged and a bigger person. You were less worried about yourself and your own affairs, and could look at yourself in relation to others."[9]

Laban used his understanding to help persons to think and make decisions for themselves. "He would never say 'You must do this, or, to achieve this, you must do that'."[10] He would never be emphatic on questions which were debatable and, in fact, seldom gave conclusive answers. He did, however, give a person the necessary experience on which to draw in order to make the decisions, which would subsequently be proved correct.

Laban would never use his understanding as a tool with which to manipulate the lives of others but he would rather employ it as an instrument which could be used by others to reach a state of self-understanding, which would allow them to fashion their own lives. When they knew themselves they would realise their own capacities and would see which was the best way for them to develop. This would lead to happiness and, as Laban says, "Happiness depends not on circumstances, but lies within us."[11]

It must not be assumed that Laban tended to dominate any situation in which he was participating. In fact, the opposite appears to be the case. He tended to be "very still in company, and just sit and listen. This could frighten until you became acquainted with him."[12] To people who never got to know him very well this may have been very disconcerting, and to some people he must have appeared "rather remote."[13] This detachment or remoteness might underlie the following remark by someone who "felt uncomfortable in his presence . . . and did not like him."[14] The reasons for this remark are, of course, open to one's individual interpretation but in this particular case Laban obviously failed to establish any *rapport*. Conversely, Wise says the thing which he remembers about Laban is "the ease with which he established relationships."[15] Tashamira also remembers that he was "sensitive in dealing with individuals and in relation to any group of people with which he finds himself confronted,"[16] while Wethered says:

"... he had an uncanny faculty of knowing how to handle people individually while directing a group, or in a private session. It was amazing what he could get out of people. With wide-open eyes he would take in everything and be ready immediately to make use of what he had seen and go on to develop from there. He was able to be with a group, feeling and experiencing with them at the same time being the observer and leader."[17]

Laban was able to observe and understand the needs of the individual within any group, realise the natural conflicts and agreements arising from the particular situation and guide the group to an experience of harmony. According to Jordan, Laban was "a magnificent choreographer"[18] and most of his best dances were based "on his knowledge of relationships in movement."[19]

A remark that "the man impressed him more than the theory"[20] suggests that the theories behind Laban's work were a little too abstract or complex, or both, for the comparatively uninitiated to understand or to apply. This could in turn imply that Laban, through his life-long study of movement, had become some sort of mystic, magician or sorcerer and his thinking had somehow become divorced from reality. In fact, Wigman,[21] Algo[22] and Terpis[23] refer to him in these terms. Laban's theories were so far in advance of their time as to appear supernatural. "Eventually the 'magician' in him overwhelmed my judgment and I came to believe him."[24] Warren Lamb says: "the element of mysticism . . . is unfortunate, for there is a great potential in Laban's work in straightforward movement observation and in learning objectively to understand what you see."[25] In addition, Valerie Preston-Dunlop says: "Work is being done to provide the necessary data to test the validity of his theories, and the results so far are proving exciting and complimentary to what must be regarded as inspired observation on Laban's part."[26]

Laban's real concern was the application of his theories to help people "fulfil themselves."[27] There is no doubt that Laban's theories are complex but "people tend to make Laban too complicated. He was always after simplicity."[28] Some of his disciples make it too complex, probably through lack of real understanding of his principles, while others will persist in dividing his work into watertight compartments and claim for each of these sections benefits which only come from a complete study of the art of movement. They seem to forget that the study of the art of movement, or any branch of it—if a branch is all that they can undertake—is not the end but a means to the end of helping people. No matter in which field of human life his theories are applied, whether it be industry, education or therapy, it is the application which is important, for the theories themselves only assume a positive and therefore beneficial impact when they are applied. Lisa Ullmann maintained that Laban believed in the power of action—positive thinking and action. Negative things are death.

The emphasis of Laban's own work clearly illustrates his belief in the power of positive action whilst its scope shows how he "constantly searched for and found relationships between previously separate aspects of movement."[29] As a result of his own experience Laban posed hypotheses "on the cosmic nature of movement, and therefrom on the interdependence of spatial and dynamic facets of motion, and on the psychophysical bases of them."[30] Many of these hypotheses are still not proven but, because "Laban was a catalyst, and herein lies much of his strength for he was a man who needed people to pursue the lines of work he started,"[31] his inspiration has been the basis of the work of Knust, Hutchinson, Szentpal (movement notation), Reber, Lange (dance ethnology), North, Lamb and Bartinieff (effort analysis).

A number of people have mentioned Laban's charm, dignity and kindness. That he had charm is shown clearly by the way most people responded to him. Loeb says that Laban demonstrated his kindness by his

> ". . . life-long friendship and interest in my work[32] . . . Laban was always trhilled when he could hear what one could do and how one could help through movement, so it went on until he died. An old friend, Father of Movement and Dance, friend of my late husband, my children and all my pupils and friends. May I add that Laban gave me my studies 'gratis.' Two years ago I gave the Centre a hall so that students can enjoy Laban's theories."[33]

How else can kindness be shown other than in a positive way? Kindness is action which stems from positive thought and a genuine desire to help.

It must not be assumed that Laban was a man who was always preoccupied with only those things in life which are associated with a grim face and a complete involvement in the serious business of living. He had a marked sense of humour which he used to good effect, both for amusing others and instructing them. Mary Wigman has the following to say on the subject:

> "What a wonderful time we had watching him, when he was in one of his humorous moods! With a flicker of an eye he seemed to take in every funny detail of a movement, a picture, a person or a given situation, and combining them with a few characteristic gestures change anything and everything into burlesque. We could not get enough of it."[34]

This shows how Laban could use his powers of understanding in a less serious way. However, the difference between burlesque and caricature is not great and Laban did use the latter with marked effect. Wigman remembers that Laban would often draw the "most vivid and often cruel caricatures. They were brilliantly done. Like a glaring flashlight they pointed out your own weak spots to you, and this in a more direct and more convincing way than any other criticism could have done. In facing them one learned a lot about one's own dear self."[35] Laban's sense of humour had a "touch of pungency to it."[36] This feeling must surely have been shared by the people in the following situations. Gertrud Snell-Friedburg had been left in charge of the Laban school timetable in Würzburg. She wrote repeatedly to Laban for the answers to questions which she did not dare decide for herself. Finally, she sent all her questions in the form of a questionnaire. Her questionnaire was returned in three days, all questions answered, but with an additional question added by Laban: "No. 18. Is Snell a silly goose? Yes! Laban."[37]

Laban, while at a meeting with the heads of one of the largest firms in England, was being questioned on the possibilities of assessing the capabilities of the staff, and how to make the best use of these capabilities.

> "At the close of the meeting one of the brighter of those present shook the meeting by suggesting that Laban had assessed them all and knew all their faults. However, Laban, with his deep sense of humour, was able to put them all at ease by quietly intimating that he never assessed the capabilities of anyone unless he was being paid for it."[38]

Laban believed deeply in the value of his work[39] and possessed an indefatigable curiosity. Wigman says: "Every new phenomenon was looked at with equal curiosity only to be jammed into one big bag, where it had to stay to be studied, to be analysed, to be worked on later."[40] The belief that Laban had in the value of his work came from years of studying movement; such a study would never have been undertaken if Laban had not been curious about the significance and the meaning of movement. These two qualities are therefore interrelated and I think it would be impossible to say which came first.

What impression of Laban comes from his own writings? In the first copy of the *Laban Art of Movement Guild Magazine*, published 1st April 1948, which was founded to perpetuate his work, Laban stated:

> "The first condition of my collaboration is, that you must grant me the privilege to try, and to err, because trial and error is the basis of all healthy development."

These are not the words of a man who was satisfied with the extent of his knowledge. They imply that he was going to continue to work and explore, and make mistakes, but that he was going to carry on working despite, or because of, his mistakes. The forward-looking implication of these words is reinforced by Gleisner, who, after listing Laban's past achievements, said, "he never rested, he always moved—and is still moving—on and on."[41] This was written when Laban was 75 years old. Laban always moved on and on despite setbacks and this could have indicated:

> ". . . his philosophy that one must never give up . . . Even if everything one had worked a lifetime to achieve were destroyed one should take a deep breath and start again, cheerfully. Laban told her that his life's work had been to collect notes on natural movement based on his own observations and he had been setting down many steps and movements to be used in various ballets. All his manuscripts were destroyed during the war when his house was burned to the ground. He immediately started writing from the beginning again."[42]

A further implication of the words in the previous paragraph is that Laban did not pretend to know all the answers as far as movement was concerned. In fact, he said, "We have found many clues, but no real answers to the question: what is the effective content of a communal group dance?"[43] We know that Laban had been greatly concerned with group dance during his years in Germany, yet he could not, or would not, state categorically which important elements to stress in such dance situations. Kurt Jooss, his close associate for many years, said that "it was characteristic of Laban's teachings never to give concrete answers."[44] Just as Laban continued to move on and on, so he wanted his pupils to do likewise, and if he gave a concrete answer this might result in a restriction instead of a constant expansion of his ideas and work. By never giving a definite solution Laban left the door open for research, but he also left it open for confusion. Laban believed that by experience and understanding of the art of movement the individual would be able to live a full and harmonious life. Once his personal guidance was gone, each person, not having Laban's width of vision, could only see his own work in isolation. Laban implied that even in isolation a person must pursue his own enquiry and that he ought to seek communication with others. Indeed he hoped that by collaborating with people concerned with different aspects of the art of movement, unification would ensue. It seems certain that he never gave concrete answers for two reasons:

1. Many of his own solutions had been modified by subsequent research and it was therefore impossible for him to say "this is right and all else is wrong."
2. He believed that the end product was not really as important as the experience which preceded the conclusion.

The first copy of the *Laban Art of Movement Guild Magazine* contained these words written by Laban: "The Guild shall not undertake any profit-making courses or schools or enterprises of any kind, nor shall it directly advertise any special method."[45] This statement suggests that there is no such thing as a Laban method of presenting dance. Laban himself did not use *a* method and, according to Lamb, "was against any system in his work."[46] This does not imply that Laban did not have his own way of broadening the movement experience of a class but he "thought that the writing down of his system might destroy the essence of his teachings."[47] Laban probably felt that to write down his own personal way of teaching would inevitably lead to a situation in which the material was more important than the class. Whilst he was against *a* method of presentation, he did see the need for a methodical foundation on which the teacher could base his interpretation of Laban's theories.

> "Modern dance is based on the large range of contemporary movement, and the best way of giving the teacher a methodical foundation on which to build up the details of his tuition had to be developed through many years.
>
> Instead of sets of standardised exercises, basic movement themes and their combinations and variations have proved to be the most helpful tool for the teacher of the contemporary form of dance.
>
> The leading idea is that the teacher should find his own manner of stimulating the pupil or classes to move, and later to dance, by choosing from a collection of basic movement themes those variations which are appropriate to the actual stage and state of development of a pupil or of the majority of a class."[48]

The above statement clearly indicates that each teacher is recommended to use the movement themes in *Modern Educational Dance* as the framework on which to build his teaching of dance. If Laban had set down a method of teaching he would have gone directly against the individuality of each person, which he had spent his life trying to develop. He wanted people to continue thinking about and experimenting with movement. He wanted each person to interpret his theories in a highly individualistic way, and the two statements just quoted could well be interpreted as a plea for countless other studies and investigations of movement. He wanted his theories and findings to be regarded as the first steps along the road to understanding the significance of movement, and not as the final definitive word on the subject.

As Laban himself may not have used a method in the teaching of dance, or movement, is it then permissible for other teachers of movement to use one? A method is used to achieve the most beneficial results in the shortest possible time, and surely every teacher wants to do this. As a teacher's experience increases, the direct paths to certain points are learned, and the way in which material is presented is refined so that as great an impact as possible is made on the children. If a teacher did not learn from his experience then his ability as a teacher would never progress from the first day that he stood in front of a class. We all use our own highly personal method. The danger of this occurs when a teacher becomes concerned with maintaining the methodological *status quo* and does not continue to refine and distil his approach in the light of his ever-widening experience, and the particular needs of his class.

What conclusions can we draw about Laban? If it is possible to reduce such a man to words, I would say that above all else he was a man of understanding. He understood man as he was, and wanted to help man to reach a state of happiness through the application of his theories on the art of movement. All the other qualities which Laban possessed sprang from this gift of understanding. He could understand the individual person and the group and could and did help each towards fulfilment. As an example of this he once said, "If you saw several of my students dance you would never guess that they were trained by the same man."[49]

REFERENCES

1. No. 2, Questionnaire, Appendix II, p. 121.
2. No. 3, Personal Interview, Appendix II, p. 127.
3. *Laban Art of Movement Guild Magazine*, December 1954, p. 16.
4. Guest, Letter, *see* Appendix II, p. 129.
5. No. 3, Interview, Appendix II, pp. 127–128.
6. *Ibid.*, p. 127.
7. Lamb, Interview, Appendix II, p. 125.
8. Garner, Questionnaire, Appendix II, p. 120.
9. Jordan, Interview, Appendix II, p. 125.
10. Dunn, Interview, Appendix II, p. 124.
11. *Laban Art of Movement Guild Magazine*, December 1954, p. 24.
12. Stephenson, Interview, Appendix II, p. 126.
13. Osmaston, Questionnaire, Appendix II, p. 121.
14. Wilson, Questionnaire, Appendix II, p. 121.
15. Wise, Questionnaire, Appendix II, p. 122.
16. *Laban Art of Movement Guild Magazine*, December 1954, p. 17.
17. Wethered, Questionnaire, Appendix II, p. 121.
18. Jordan, Personal Interview, Appendix II, p. 125.
19. *Ibid.*, p. 125.

20. Wise, Questionnaire, Appendix II, p. 122.
21. *Laban Art of Movement Guild Magazine*, December 1954, p. 6.
22. *Ibid.*, p. 14.
23. *Ibid.*, p. 18.
24. Preston-Dunlop, Letter, Appendix II, p. 132.
25. Lamb, Interview, Appendix II, pp. 125–126.
26. Preston-Dunlop, *Journal of the Physical Education Association*, July 1967, p. 50.
27. Dunn, Interview, Appendix II, p. 123.
28. Stephenson, Interview, *see* Appendix II, p. 126.
29. Preston-Dunlop, *Journal*, July 1967, p. 49.
30. *Ibid.*, p. 49.
31. *Ibid.*, p. 50.
32. Loeb, Questionnaire, Appendix II, p. 121.
33. Loeb, Letter, Appendix, p. 130.
34. *Laban Art of Movement Guild Magazine*, December 1954, p. 6.
35. *Ibid.*, p. 6.
36. Wise, Questionnaire, Appendix II, p. 122.
37. *Laban Art of Movement Guild Magazine*, December 1954, p. 19.
38. *Ibid.*, p. 25.
39. Metcalfe and contributor, No. 1, Questionnaire, Appendix II, pp. 121 and 120.
40. *Laban Art of Movement Guild Magazine*, December 1954, p. 15.
41. *Ibid.*, p. 15.
42. Garner, Questionnaire, Appendix II, p. 120.
43. *Laban Art of Movement Guild Magazine*, March 1955, p. 15.
44. *Ibid.*, December 1954, p. 15.
45. *Ibid.*, April 1948, p. 7.
46. Lamb, Interview, Appendix II, p. 125.
47. Stephenson, Interview, Appendix II, p. 126.
48. R. Laban: *Modern Educational Dance*, p. 27.
49. No. 3, Interview, Appendix II, p. 127.

Chapter 3

The Philosophy of Rudolf Laban

The philosophy of Rudolf Laban is extremely complex and his many books relating to movement scarcely do justice to his beliefs. Nowhere is there a philosophy explicitly set out and his publications in German are as difficult to elucidate as are those appearing in English. Obviously this account of his philosophy will fall short, but the attempt is necessary if we require some estimate of his contribution to movement and of the application of his ideas to education.

Rather than lose the reader in the ramifications of Laban's thoughts, attention is drawn to the seven major features of his philosophy:

1. The significance of movement in the life of man.
2. Harmony in Nature and in man.
3. Natural rhythm.
4. The creative influence in the universe and in man.
5. Art as a creative force.
6. Movement, effort and communication.
7. Conflict.

1. The significance of movement in the life of man

The study of movement is vast and complicated and calls for some appreciation, from physiological, historical, ethnological and psychological standpoints, of man in his world. Essentially, such study is concerned with man's basic physical equipment on the one hand and his striving for immortality on the other.

Man's awareness of the world in which he moves comes from his perception of some of the continuous stream of stimuli from his environment. Perception depends upon the stimulation of the sense organs and Laban maintained that "all our senses are variations of our unique sense of touch."[1] When the skin is bent or deformed in some way a sensation of touch is experienced; similarly, the pressure of sound waves upon the eardrum and the impact of light waves upon the retina arouse

audible and visual sensations and underline the physical nature of man's perception. Man's kinaesthetic sense, in some ways his most important sense, is stimulated by bodily activity giving rise to an awareness of the sensation of the movement of the body. We perceive bodily relationships through our kinaesthetic sense; it is the effect of these relationships which triggers off a mental response.

Reflection will show that certain combinations of movement will lead to a definite mental reaction and this mental attitude will always be expressed by this pattern of movement. Thus, movement can affect attitude and mood and mental state is shown by movement. Throughout his life man develops his experience of movement which enables him to apply the body–mind relationship beyond himself. His mental response to the movement patterns of others can stimulate his movement and one man can arouse a great number to mental and physical activity.

It is not possible to explain all of man's life in terms of mental activity in response to physical perception. Some men's thoughts and actions have placed their physical survival in jeopardy; some have pioneered thought and development not based on any logic or climate of their age, and the stimulus to think and behave in this way cannot, therefore, be explained in terms of the attainment of mental and physical goals. The term that Laban used for this area of man's experience is "spiritual" and he equates this with man's persistent search for values, his intuition and his creative ability. Laban is not alone in his belief that there is a dimension to man which defies mathematical evaluation. His conception of life was such that he saw movement as a reciprocal link between man's mental, spiritual and physical life. Movement is more than a component of the chain which links man's inner activity and the world around him, for it is the medium through which he actualises his responses.

It is through the movement of other people and objects that man refines and expands his knowledge of the world "because our own movements and those we perceive around us are basic experiences."[2] Thus the study of movement to which Rudolf Laban devoted his whole life is essentially concerned with a person in relation to the world and the people around him.

"Looking at the whole range of the innate and acquired impulses of man, one is tempted to search for a common denominator. In my opinion this denominator is not mere motion, but movement with all its spiritual implications. In movement none of the spiritual or physical values can be left aside. The good man is he who exemplifies in his movement physical, mental and spiritual values as a unified whole. The practice of body–mind movement in all its variations has to be supplemented by a thorough research into the nature and the ramifications of movement."[3]

2. Harmony in Nature and in man

To Laban there was a natural harmony in life. He saw this in the orbiting of the stars as well as in the life of cells. In the stellar world these orbits were not mere motion but movement, for they were contributing towards the stability and harmony of the universe. When something happens to upset stellar stability, adjustments are necessary to re-establish harmony and man cannot affect either the first or subsequent event in any way.

The same situation is found in the cell-state. While each individual cell appears to be concerned only with its own functions it is inextricably concerned with the well-being of the organism as a whole. Each cell has its own part to play in the overall pattern of things. Man cannot really affect this either. He may assist them to do their jobs by the use of drugs, or remove some growth, which the cells cannot overcome, by the use of surgery, but the majority of the work must be done by the effort of the cells themselves. The maintenance of the stability and harmony of the organism is a law of Nature, according to Laban. The world of cells is visualised in personalistic terms as

". . . a long series of what might be called noble sentiments and endeavours. In the dramatic battles which these little creatures have to fight in order to defend their buildings and to secure the freedom necessary for the unhindered performance of their activities, we see a great many heroic actions, much self-sacrifice and mutual help, comparable with similar manifestations in man's social behaviour. We therefore cannot say that the central controlling mind has invented or monopolised any of these virtues or wisdoms. All the possible virtues and volitions exist, and are fulfilled in an exemplary way, in the life of cells.

> We could, of course, suppose that these noble tendencies are infiltrated from above; that is, the cells learn their pride–modesty, their capacity to be social and energetic from the examples set and the advice given by the governing cell groups; but alas, this illusion is revealed as such by the fact that the most anti-social mind often enjoys the most wonderfully harmonious and smoothly functioning cell life. Is it not more true that the anti-social governing cell-groups of a healthy and harmonious cell-state have failed to learn from their subordinates to distinguish right from wrong?"[4]

It would seem that each cell has the option to determine its own reaction to any given situation, and that the central mind plays little part in determining the way in which the cell reacts. Why then do cells normally react in a way which is to the benefit of themselves and the organism as a whole? They do so in a response which is governed by the natural law of maintaining the stability and harmony of the organism. This is his fundamental premise based on the belief that life is a positive force and wants to grow and flourish.

If, therefore, we accept that each cell is capable of differentiating between right and wrong, with respect to its own situation within the organism, then the organism should also be capable of making similar differentiations within the framework of its environment. Before any such demarcations can be made, the implication that there is such a thing as right and wrong, and the other qualities which Laban mentions, has to be accepted. Some societies have recognised and responded to the implications of this natural harmony having awareness that "the bodily perspective, with all its significance for the human personality, can have a regenerating effect on our individual and social forms of life. Through conscious and constant usage this effect can de deepened, which helps us to explain the role that dance played in certain epochs of civilisation when a notable harmony was achieved."[5]

Laban further argues that if the stability and harmony of the universe is reflected in the cell, free from the control of the central mind, then these qualities can be said to have existed before man. They are not, therefore, subject to his control, and were not initiated by him. If they are not man-made, and we accept that they do exist, from where do they originate? It is possible to deduce an answer to this question·

by the conclusion that Laban drew from an analogy based on the paths of electrons. While most electrons follow complicated but regular tracts there are some which do not obey any known physical law. These apparently exercise free will in the choice of their paths. Laban considered:

> ". . . there are only two solutions to this riddle which physicists will admit; either there are some natural laws of a completely new kind hitherto unknown, or there exists (as humbler scientists are inclined to think) some designing and controlling power behind, above or within the universe which is able and willing to perform such extravagances for the sake of unfathomable purposes."[6]

This surely indicates that Laban believed in a creator and that there was a purpose to life and to the universe.

It is acknowledged that this particular section of Laban's philosophy may well provoke some readers to say, "If this is what dance is based upon, no wonder they do the things they do!" Yet harmony does exist within man and in the natural world, and man does attempt to make this harmonic bond with his fellows. Evidence does exist for this harmony but it must be admitted that such a harmony will not, to some, be synonymous with the existence of a force which created this harmony. It should be remembered, however, that man, as a species, seems to have a need to believe in and identify with an omnipotent force or being. This need has taken many different forms during man's existence and appears to stem from man's attempt to give a purpose to his life because he knows that he will die. The fact that Laban visualises the observable harmony of nature as the force with which man can identify himself need not detract from the fundamental worth of Laban's ideas. Mutual co-operation, self-exploration and development, exercise of the choice between right and wrong, seem to be qualities of value and worthy of attention.

3. Natural rhythm

Laban believed that there was also a natural–universal rhythm as well as a natural harmony to life. He believed that this rhythm, whether it is visible in the orbits of planets or electrons, the action of the tides, the coming of the seasons, or displayed by and within man, was the manifestation of a purposive law of nature. By comparing the rhythmic orbits of matter to man's gestures he emphasised his belief in this universality.

> "In his gestures man changes the positions of his body and his limbs in space exactly as in a stylised way the electrons, atoms and molecules of matter do. So also do the stars, comets, suns, nebulae and systems of milky ways."[7]

He further illustrates the universality of rhythm in the use of freedom in space. Once again he used the analogy of the apparently free electron, but this time he linked it with those stars which suddenly, and to man for no apparent reason, leave their prescribed orbit. He saw in this the "natural" exploration and use of space. As a star leaves its orbit so the other stars compensate and take up new formations in space forming new constellations; in the world of the electron new atoms are formed, using space as the medium of establishing new rhythms.

To Laban "empty space does not exist. On the contrary, space is a superabundance of simultaneous movements,"[8] and it is through the rhythm of these movements that "the forms of objects, as well as the shapes assumed by living organisms, wax and wane uninterruptedly."[9] This waxing and waning also applies to light and sound waves, for at particular frequencies we are aware of audible or visual sensations, whilst other frequencies, above or below this optimum level, are beyond our perception.

This continuous rhythmic vibration occurs within space and to Laban "space is a hidden feature of movement and movement is a visible aspect of space."[10] Some of these rhythms are so protracted that no movement is visible and so it is assumed that a state of rest or immobility exists. No true state of immobility is possible "since matter itself is a compound of vibrations,"[11] and a concept of life in which movement is an occasional exception to the rule of stillness needs examination. Movement is only acknowledged to exist when we perceive it, yet it continues, rhythmically, whether we perceive it or not, and what is called "'equilibrium' is never complete stability or a standstill."[12] The mind, as it perceives this universal rhythm, freezes it into a series of images and creates the impression of empty space and immobile, unrelated objects, but children and primitive peoples are aware of this universal rhythm and "know" it through their physical experience and their simple, unified approach to life. To them space is not a void but is full of rhythms and movement, which they recognise as the "basic experience of existence."[13] Just as the free electrons and stars are at liberty to choose their pathways, so also is man.

> "This freedom is exactly what man feels when he chooses the paths and the rhythms for his movements in Doing and Dancing. He feels around him an enormous network of related tracks, from which he can choose those which he likes, those which seem to be adequate to his present purposes in Doing or which correspond to the expression of his inner agitation in Dancing. Not only is there a similarity between the intricate network of the paths of electrons and that of bodily movements, but also there is the same freedom of choice in the free use of unlimited tracks in a borderless space."[14]

It would seem that man, in his unsophisticated state where the mind does not impose limitations on the spontaneous use of the body, is capable of demonstrating his natural rhythm. "Animals and savages are instinctively aware of the importance of this basic rhythmical necessity; so are children."[15] Man in his sophistication, however, often allows the mind to become too dominant and imposes barriers between the body and this rhythm, for "he [man] indulges in a proud and resentful hatred of his body and thus he also hates Dancing,"[16] for dancing is the most natural way for man to display rhythm. Once this happens man is in danger of losing his meaningful and good life. Instead of imposing barriers, man should attempt to give his mind greater facility in picking up the pulses of this rhythm.

> "In listening more carefully inside he would find that in Dancing, as in Doing, there exists a formidable order and common code of laws without which life becomes meaningless, if not evil. The mind could detect that these laws were given by nature and that he as the controller–servant can do nothing but recognise and cultivate the pre-established harmony. He would see that the co-existence and co-relationship of the mind, striving after consciousness, and the basic urge of nature, creating the tangible existence of the body, cannot be severed without annihilating both life and awareness."[17]

4. Movement as a visible creative influence

Laban believed that man, through his movement, is linked with the movements of planets and matter and is part of the natural order and rhythm of the universe. He did not believe that the creator is the universe but rather that the purpose of the creator is revealed in the universe through the fundamental laws of harmony, rhythm, freedom and the choice between right and wrong. If these fundamental laws are not man-made, and there is a purpose to them, there must be some creative influence responsible for this order. To Laban the movements of the natural world were indications of the existence of this creative influence and the orbits of stars and electrons were not *motion* but *movement* since their path through space was dictated by a natural law. Similarly with man, whose actions are also *movement* since they require mental, spiritual and physical participation. Laban wrote that "the whole world is filled with unceasing movement. An unsophisticated mind has no difficulty in comprehending movement as life."[18]

It is through movement that man, whether primitive or modern, can attune himself to this natural order by the use of his body–mind movements. Primitive man achieved this through dance; modern man, because he no longer dances in a primitive way, needs to be reawakened to the consistently important role of movement in his life. Here I think is the foundation of Laban's belief in the value of movement. Research into the nature and ramifications of movement, which Laban termed the Art of Movement, can enable man to take the first steps towards fulfilling his natural purpose, and understanding the reason for his very existence. It is through movement that man can experience all of the urges which are within him, express them in a way which is natural to him and develop himself to the full. Man is given everything he needs in order to be able to express these fundamental laws but this expression can only be achieved when there is a true balance between each of the factors which combine to make man a complete person. If any one factor achieves a state of domination then the harmony is upset and true expression ceases. It is only when all aspects are given equal opportunity to develop that man will continue to prosper. Movement presents the best and the simplest opportunity for this.

The endeavours of man, whether primitive or sophisticated,

can be divided into those activities which are directed towards the maintenance of his life and those which are devoid of any such obvious purpose. Laban defined these two basic characteristics of man's life as "Doing" and "Dancing."

> "Doing is purposeful and may be understood as signifying all action by which practical aims are pursued. Doing is thus distinguished from Dancing in which the aims pursued appear to the great number of our contemporaries as superfluous, or at least of secondary importance. Dancing is not, however, unnecessary for the actual preservation of life, although it seems devoid of any practical purpose. But equally purposeless are all the other arts and spiritual endeavours, which we know today have actually originated from dancing. All these leisure activities, including the joyful play of children, are entirely inessential to the simple preservation of life, but they are essential in the recovery from the strain of doing.
>
> The purposeful struggle of ordinary doing prevails in work. All our Doing in work with its exciting competition and its hazardous uncertainties and fancies has more than one trait in common with dancing and playing. Doing and Dancing have moreover a common instrument in the body, and a common medium in movement directed by thought and emotion."[19]

Since movement is the visible manifestation of the natural creative force, man, through a study of the art of movement, will come nearer to an understanding of the fundamentals of life in his work and in his leisure.

When man seeks reality through purely intellectual activity and ignores movement, he is divorcing himself from the physical world and is losing his true perspective of life.

> "Man of later time loses this view through reflective delusions and also because of his increasing tactile incapacity. He establishes stability in his mind as a contrasting partner to mobility. In this way he becomes unrelated to his surroundings which are, in the widest sense, the universe, and thus he loses his personality."[20]

Movement is a medium for actualising one's place and one's purpose in the cosmos and to Laban it was more than a way of educating man. He believed that it was *the* way of educating through the arts and that dance, demanding as it does the full involvement of the mental, physical and spiritual abilities of man, "is the primary art of man."[21]

5. Movement as a creative art

Art to Laban was the visible representation of the sublime qualities of man and he thought of dance or dancing as more than the most basic expressive medium of man. To Laban it was an art. "Dance as an Art form has become one of the rarest and most admired flowers of civilised life."[22] True art cannot be achieved without the conscious application of the mind in solving the problems of the world in which man lives. Laban held that art, presenting as it does the most complex problems, has not only drawn the best from the mind, but through the presentation of such complex problems, has contributed towards the efficiency of the mind, for he said, "the functioning of the human mind would not be what it is without the arts."[23]

Dance demands the involvement of all the faculties of man and Laban held that dance as an art activated the mind by sharpening man's mental apparatus as it requires the creation of new and meaningful movement patterns communicating relationships between man, his fellows and his environment. Before this is possible the artist needs to gain an understanding of the flow of movement and a real awareness of pathways through space; he will experiment with time and contend with gravity. The artist absorbs the experiences arising from the movement of the world around him, the feelings and emotions of his fellows and then describes them kinaesthetically. This is possible because of the vast movement memory and understanding of the artist. Finally all this personal and external experience is synthesised, selected and organised to produce those original statements which demark art from creative experience, and which demand a total absorption of mind and body.

The artist is a man apart using his material to the limits but this same material can be used creatively by all. The art of movement, using the body as its medium of expression, is unique in that there are no external tools to master. It provides opportunity for a person "to develop his own approach and use his own interpretation."[24] Knowledge of the components of movement gives experience of a person's natural rhythm and allows freedom of choice. Man chooses certain pathways for his movement in space and these pathways which outline the shape of movement Laban calls "trace forms." If pathways are badly chosen, through lack of experience or the attitude of the moving person, disharmony will be experienced and the sequence will possess an unreal quality. The study and practice of the relationships inherent in "trace forms" open the way to an experience of harmony and creativity through movement. All this is within the capabilities of all men, for Laban believed that "the field of individual movement creativeness is to a greater or smaller extent open to everybody."[25]

That everyone wants to attain a goal is a common belief and a study of the art of movement would allow a person to experience this feeling of attainment, for it presents challenges which are within the compass of everyone to overcome. It also allows a person to produce something either by himself or with others, which is unique. After the improvisation and exploration stage at least four considerations seem to be of importance:

1. There must be at some stage in the process a concept of what the finished product will be.
2. There must be the intention to achieve this.
3. Knowledge of and familiarity with the body (the medium of expression) are essential.
4. It will be necessary to be adept at handling the tools which are suitable to this medium.

In dance, with its precise vocabulary of expression, it is possible to reach a certain degree of pre-comprehension as to the form of the end product; as dance is also the most basic form of artistic expression it is the most natural way for man to be creative.

6. Movement, effort, expression and communication

Movement is not the mere motion of limbs and body in some haphazard way divorced from inner participation; it is the visible manifestation of man's true intellectual, emotional and spiritual state and "is the result of striving after an object deemed valuable, or of a state of mind."[26] It is the link between man's intentions and their realisation through action. This link, between the covert and the overt behaviour of man, Laban termed *the flow of movement* which "fills all our functions and actions; it discharges us from detrimental inner tensions."[27]

Movement may be deliberately or unconsciously expressive and *shadow* movements, "the tiny movements of muscles which have no other than expressive value; such as twitches and jerks of the face and hand,"[28] are particularly revealing of an inner state of conflict or serenity.

The inner impulse, which gives rise to movement, Laban called *effort*[29] and every effort can be regarded as being made up of four *factors*: Space, Weight, Time and Flow. The effort characteristics of each person are unique and his movement will show the effect of his heredity and environment. These same efforts, visibly displayed in the rhythms of man's bodily motion are used during his expressive, objective and recreational activities and the way in which the factors are indulged in or fought against is remarkably consistent. Effort is involved in every voluntary and involuntary movement; therefore to understand movement it is necessary to comprehend the effort life of man.

In order to acquire a rich effort life, which will lead to the development of expression and communication, it is necessary to turn to the medium of dance, for in dance we can recognise "an organised co-operation of our mental, emotional and bodily powers resulting in actions the experience of which is of the greatest importance to the development of the . . . personality."[30] Through dance it is possible to participate in situations which are outside a person's normal effort experience and discipline is acquired, for dance "makes expression precise, and therefore better understandable for our neighbours."[31]

A heightened awareness of movement should lead to an appreciation of one's own movement and the movement of others and a recognition of the significance of both deliberate and unconscious movements. Such awareness is necessary because movement "is the means of communication between people, because all our forms of expression—speaking, writing, singing—are carried by the flow of movement."[32]

7. Conflict

To Laban man is in constant conflict:

> "We never know whether man regards himself as taking part in a tragedy or a comedy with himself as the protagonist in the drama of existence and Nature forming the chorus. Yet it is an

undeniable fact that man's extraordinary power of thought and action has placed him in a peculiar situation so far as his relationship to his surroundings is concerned. Man tries to enact the conflicts arising from the solitary role of his race."[33]

He portrays the conflicts "arising from human striving after material, emotional and spiritual values."[34] By a study of body–mind movement Laban hoped that it was possible for man to resolve some of these conflicts and thus achieve an integrated personality and a full awareness of his relationship and responsibilities to the natural world.

In psychological terms the integration of personality is accomplished through a harmonious development of body and mind. Laban considered the purpose of "body–mind movement" was to give

> ". . . an experience of the reconciliation between the often antagonistic inner trends of man, and to provide this experience is one of the main aims of recreation through the art of movement, not only for the stage dancer, but for everybody. Well applied, such exercise can have a lasting effect on the integration of personality."[35]

Laban considered that the antagonistic trends arose mainly in the conflict of emotional demands and rational requirements. Obviously, a first requirement is that a person must fully comprehend his own rational and emotional response to any given situation, for when these are reinforcing each other a state of harmony will exist, but when they are opposed, disharmony is the result.

Laban's aims, by the application of his theories on the art of movement, were to help a person to reach a more accurate understanding of himself, and, through this, a better understanding of others. By means of this understanding of others there would be a greater facility for forming good human relationships; and by the creation of situations, at work and leisure, an individual would be able fully to realise his own capabilities.

If man is to have conditions of work which are as congenial as possible he must try to find an occupation in which he will be able to use movements which are most natural to him. Before such a work situation can arise it must be understood that everyone has an optimum field of employment which will give him satisfaction. In order to facilitate the setting up of such a situation, Laban studied objectively the subjective movement habits of others, whether or not these movement habits were successful.

> "The aim of this study was to create for the average person (child, adolescent or adult) the possibility of gaining a certain degree of satisfaction in both work and leisure-time activities by matching the form of his activity with his available capacity."[36]

When movement is studied from the seven major points of Laban's philosophy it becomes a study of man in his entirety and not a mere study of motion. All movement, to the skilled movement observer, is significant but to reach such a comprehensive understanding of the significance of movement is a long process. However, a start can be made in attempting to understand this significance by studying the works of Rudolf Laban. No longer are we satisfied with accurate observation of overt behaviour; we want to know more about the covert behaviour which precedes it. In short, we are no longer solely concerned with what man does with movement but we are becoming increasingly aware of what movement does to man.

REFERENCES

1. R. Laban: *Choreutics*, p. 29.
2. *Ibid.*, p. 3.
3. *Laban Art of Movement Guild Magazine*, November 1958, p. 12.
4. *Ibid.*, May 1959, pp. 8 and 9.
5. R. Laban: *Choreutics*, p. 8.
6. *Laban Art of Movement Guild Magazine*, May 1959, p. 16.
7. *Ibid.*, May 1959, p. 13.
8. R. Laban: *Choreutics*, p. 3.
9. *Ibid.*, p. 3.
10. *Ibid.*, p. 4.
11. *Ibid.*, p. 4.
12. *Ibid.*, p. 6.
13. *Ibid.*, p. 6.
14. *Laban Art of Movement Guild Magazine*, May 1959, p. 17.
15. *Ibid.*, p. 10.
16. *Ibid.*, p. 10.

17. *Ibid.*, p. 10.
18. R. Laban: *Choreutics*, p. 6.
19. *Laban Art of Movement Guild Magazine*, May 1959, pp. 6 and 7.
20. R. Laban, *Choreutics*, p. 6.
21. *Laban Art of Movement Guild Magazine*, May 1959, p. 6.
22. *Ibid.*, p. 6.
23. *Ibid.*, p. 6.
24. R. Laban: *Modern Educational Dance*, p. 51.
25. *Laban Art of Movement Guild Magazine*, March 1955, p. 16.
26. R. Laban: *The Mastery of Movement on the Stage*, p. 2.
27. R. Laban: *Modern Educational Dance*, p. 95.
28. R. Laban: *The Mastery of Movement on the Stage*, p. 12.
29. *Ibid.*, p. 11.
30. R. Laban: *Modern Educational Dance*, p. 43.
31. *Ibid.*, p. 96.
32. *Ibid.*, p. 95.
33. R. Laban: *The Mastery of Movement on the Stage*, p. 5.
34. *Ibid.*, p. 103.
35. *Laban Art of Movement Guild Magazine*, March 1954, p. 8.
36. *Ibid.*, November 1957, p. 13.

Chapter 4

Principles of Movement

To attempt to outline the principles of movement on which depend the practice of movement is not an easy task. Many people will not even admit to the existence of movement principles whilst others, when questioned, quote examples of practical work and not the fundamental issues of movement. By reading Laban's works I have been able to deduce two principles of movement but I would hasten to point out that nowhere in the works of Rudolf Laban are his principles of movement presented in a way which makes constant and repeated reference easy. It is a characteristic of his writings that he leaves the reader to draw his own conclusions and I would like, therefore, to re-emphasise that the principles of movement which are enumerated here are my interpretaions gained from studying his works:

1. Movement enables man to realise his physical potential.
2. Movement characterises man.

1. Movement enables man to realise his physical potential

The days of regarding the body as a necessary evil to be scourged and mutilated are long since gone, but the idea that an outstanding physical ability is in some way inferior to, and not as significant as, an academic ability still persists. Even though many people would rather develop an intellectual potential, in preference to a physical potential, because of the need to earn a living, it should not be forgotten that man has a physical dimension which deserves as much consideration and attention as the other aspects of his being. Man, in his infancy, learned about himself and the world around him by his physical sensations and bodily movement. By body-training and movement awareness, man, in his adult state, can still gain valuable experience of himself and his environment. Immense satisfaction and a feeling of achievement will be gained from training his body and finding the right outlet for his physical make-up, be it football, archery or dancing. This search for physical proficiency will also show him his weaknesses and limitations; giving him the opportunity to face realities, strive for that which is within his reach. This seeking will very soon give him insight into the fact that there is more to man's movement than the exercising of his muscles and few would deny that the workings of the mind and the functioning of the body have very positive interactions and interconnections.

> "Movement can be studied like any other reality of existence. One can see its mechanical implications, coming from the instrumental character of our body. The parts of our skeleton are levered by muscles in a way not dissimilar from the function of a mobile crane with which we lift and transport merchandise. But in the crane sits a master-mind, the crane-driver, who organises the motions of the crane, enabling this contraption to serve a definite job. We can know all about every single screw and pulley of the crane without being able to drive it by our thinking only. For the driving we need movement.
>
> The body is crane and crane-driver in one well-assembled unit, and this unit follows—knowingly or unknowingly—the invariable rules of bodily and mental motion."[1]

2. Movement characterises man

Movement, even to the relatively unskilled observer, may be unconsciously or deliberately expressive and in either case it can be analysed into the *motion factors* in terms of its strength or lightness (*Weight*), its directness or flexibility (*Space*), its suddenness or sustainment (*Time*) and its bound or free quality (*Flow*). It was a person's attitude to these four components of movement that Laban called *effort.* The shape and rhythm of movement "shows a special attitude to meet the situation in which the action takes place. It can characterise the momentary mood, or the personality of the moving person,"[2] and those unconsciously expressive movements, such as the way of walking, sitting or using the hands while talking, make each person readily distinguishable from his neighbour. This cannot be otherwise, for each person has a mental and physical make-up which is unique, and movement, being a compound of mental and physical involvement, is bound to be highly individualistic. Even within those situations in which there are highly prescribed ways of operating, the movement patterns will display in some manner the individual's characteristics which can be analysed in terms of effort. The movement patterns of Bobby Charlton, George Best and Denis Law, and their responses to the situations which occur on the soccer field, show the effort rhythms of their distinctive styles of play.

Any task or situation demands certain things of those engaged upon the task whose abilities and potentials will certainly affect the way in which the task is fulfilled. "Some people have a natural vocation for certain tasks. Put on work which is consonant with their gifts, they will show an admirable economy of effort, and this is the first prerequisite of skill."[3] The converse is also true where inappropriate tasks or personnel will result in much wasted and futile effort. The performance of any activity is controlled to some extent by physical build and attitude. Inhibition, anxiety, fear and self-consciousness are aspects of an unsatisfactory attitude to a situation. Laban believed that

> "... the prevailing action character and its shadings can be observed either in the reactions of a person to specific situations, or in his or her habitual movements.
>
> Certain reactions will be quite improbable, or at least exceptional, but rarely entirely impossible. We can hardly expect a relatively weak or slow person to be heroic or quick except in exceptional circumstances.
>
> Here we reach a crucial point, *viz.*, the possibility of the change in habitual effort make-up. Slow changes can be promoted through experience gained in everyday life, but certain lopsided effort-capacities may be so ingrained that it is very difficult to change them."[4]

It is possible to overcome most of these often self-imposed limitations through greater understanding of the person who is affected by them, and it is in this field that Laban's work is so valuable. Laban maintained that "two main kinds of obstruction are possible; the physical and the mental inhibition,"[5] and his specific principles of movement were directed towards breaking down these two inhibitions.

Man is not always inhibited about his use of movement. He can and does use movement as a very obvious and positive way of expressing his emotions. Indeed some maintain that true expression begins where language ends and a profound emotional experience is often beyond words. Without movement there would be no outlet for any of the experiences which man undergoes.

The arts mirror these experiences and some of the arts use movement in a consciously expressive way. During a concert a conductor's movements are his only means of communicating with the orchestra and the patterns traced by his arms and his whole body movements do more than set the rhythm and tempo of the work; they convey to the orchestra the "feeling" that he wants the orchestra to project. The movement of actors may be said to be aimed at augmenting the impact of the spoken word so that the audible and visual aspects of their character have a unity. It is not that movement is tailored to fit the words but rather that movement and speech, indicative of a state of mind, have a unity in the way in which they project this attitude. The dancer strives for understanding and control of his body since his only means of expression and communication is his movement. The transient nature of dance is such that dancers need constantly to broaden and deepen their own movement experience. They need technique to help them master their body and the ideal technique is one of overall awareness and not a series of exercises. Dancers should consistently return to the ultimate source material for dance which is movement; movement that is observed, enjoyed for its own sake or used in situations other than dance in order to create beauty, both for performer and spectator, and contribute to an appreciation of dance as an expressive, creative medium.

Laban's second general principle of movement offers him a means of helping mankind through a study and analysis of movement. Such a study is an attempt to refine our thinking about movement in Nature. The strength of Laban's analysis is that it is interpreted in terms of human beings rather than Newtonian physics. Perhaps Laban had been impressed by the uninhibited movement of animals and savages and been drawn to a "naturalistic" basis for his study of movement. His view of the cosmos supports this interpretation and it is not surprising that he looked to natural philosophy for illumination. In the field of physics there was an established analysis of motion, but he wished to go beyond Newtonian physics.[6]

His interpretation of movement includes mechanical analysis

but adds more, for he is concerned with *effort* which meant to Laban, as earlier indicated, the "attitudes of the moving person to the motion factors of Weight, Space, Time and Flow."[7] It should not be assumed that because the word "effort" is, in everyday language, associated with strenuous activity that the same applies in movement. On the contrary, effort can be as easily displayed through comparatively small muscular activity as through a great amount of body movement. Whether movements are large or small they will consistently reveal which of the motion factors are predominantly influential. No person can be exclusively addicted to one motion factor since movements, and therefore efforts, "are bound to evolve in space as well as in time."[8] Strong, direct and sudden movements struggle against Weight, Space and Time, whilst light, flexible and sustained movements indulge these motion factors. It is the way in which Weight, Space, Time and Flow are used which gives each effort its distinctive power, shape, duration and rhythm.

Laban's fourth motion factor is Flow and movements in which "free flow" is evident will look and feel quite different from those subject to "bound flow"—where the movement can be stopped at any required instant. It is possible to distinguish this flow element, whether bound or free, and it is present in movement "whatever velocity, space expansion or force the movement might have."[9] Even when the Space, Weight and Time factors remain the same, to "free" or "bind" the flow of a movement has a significant effect on its character and appearance. Bound flow movements need not be cramped, either spatially or in their use of force, nor need they be predominantly quick or slow; similarly free flow movements can be accomplished "without necessarily giving much attention to the various shades of time, weight and the space development of the movement."[10] The Flow factor seems to display an attitude to the whole movement and not one particular aspect of it, and even though the Flow of a movement is usually governed by the factors of Space, Weight and Time, this need not always be the case. Since the Flow factor is capable of influencing movement, quite independently of the other three motion factors, it is not a second order factor as might be thought, because "persons do not move either suddenly or deliberately, weakly or forcefully, flexibly or directly only."[11]

As a result of empirical observation Laban named the eight basic efforts Dabbing, Flicking, Floating, Gliding, Pressing, Punching, Slashing and Wringing, but it should be remembered that these verbal terms are used "for the approximate description of effort contents without being able to adhere strictly to their everyday meaning."[12] The way in which these basic efforts use the motion factors is diagrammatically represented on page 34 of *Modern Educational Dance*, a reproduction of which appears in Fig. 1.

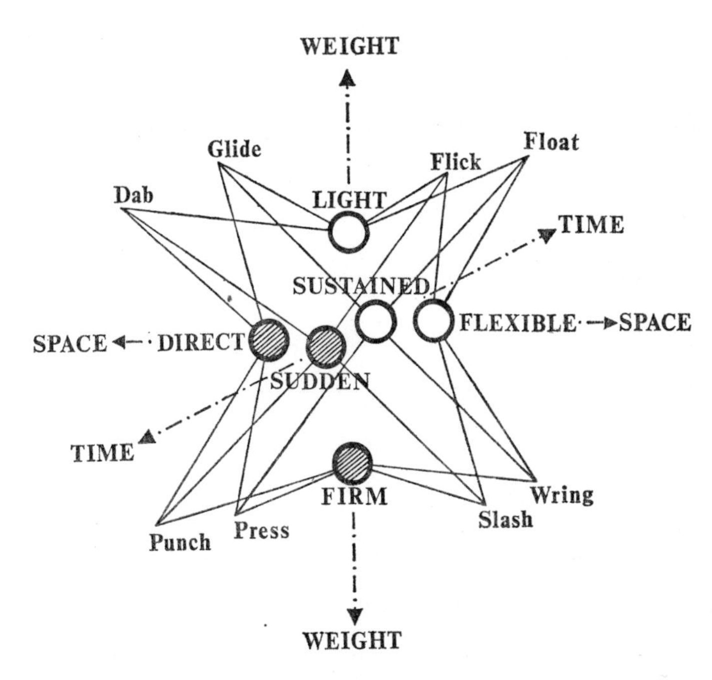

Fig. 1. The six effort elements and the eight basic effort actions. Shaded circles show elements fighting against, while open circles show elements indulging in, Weight or Space or Time.

Laban also summarised relationships between the basic efforts on pages 24 and 25 of *Effort.* In Fig. 2 those efforts connected by a line have two motion factors in common and the line indicates the motion factor to be altered if an effort change is required. Efforts which are connected in this way, by the change of one motion factor, *e.g.* Wringing and Pressing, are said to be primarily akin.

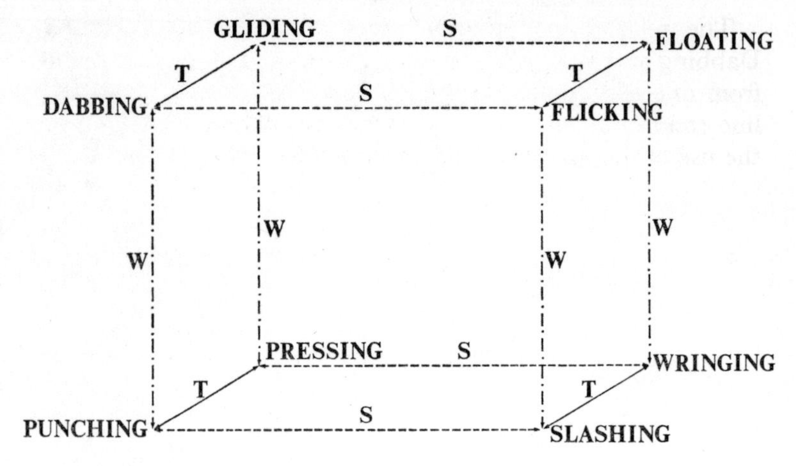

FIG. 2. Primarily akin effort actions.

Efforts are secondarily akin when they have one motion factor in common and differ in two, *e.g.* Punching and Gliding as shown in Fig. 3. The lines indicate which of the efforts are related in this way and also the motion factors which have to be altered if such an effort change is necessary.

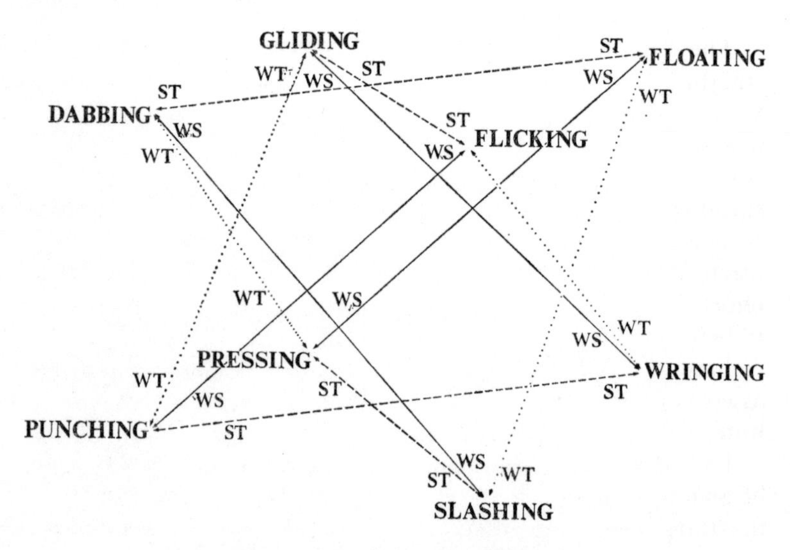

FIG. 3. Secondarily akin effort actions.

The relationship between pairs of contrasting efforts, *e.g.* Dabbing and Wringing, is summarised in Fig. 4. The change from one effort to its contrast, indicated in the diagram by a line connecting the two, can only be accomplished by altering the use of the Space, Weight and Time motion factors.

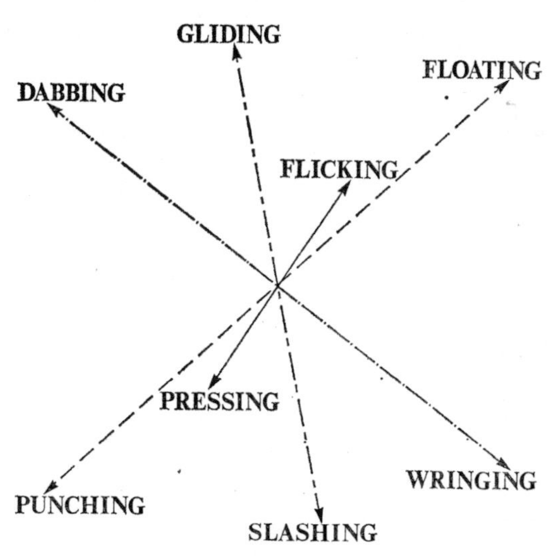

FIG. 4. Contrasting effort actions

The importance which Laban attached to effort understanding is quite categorically stated as is his view that effort-training has significance for man's development. "Once rightly assessed, individual effort can be changed and improved by training, for, in the end, all education is based upon effort-training."[13] Effort assessment, effort-training and education through effort awareness can only be attempted after a protracted course of study and such a profound knowledge of effort is a complex technique in its own right. It is not enough to believe whole-heartedly in the significance of effort and "the rudimentary knowledge of a principle is not sufficient for the assessment of a person's aptitude for special work or for guiding him to the right choice of profession."[14]

To Laban, effort was visibly displayed through the rhythms of man's bodily motion and to understand man it is necessary to study the components of these rhythms. From this one naturally concludes that for a man to understand himself he must be aware of his own efforts, by realising the use he makes of the motion factors. Any such self-analysis is likely to be a crude one and usually needs supporting or delineating by more experienced observers. It is only by effort training that we can break the stranglehold of those automatic effort rhythms which have become stereotyped through constant repetition. Such stereotyped responses, often for reasons of which we are unaware, hinder our development as people, since we are only dimly conscious of ourselves.

"In general effort-training stress is laid on the awakening of the bodily feel of the co-ordination of motion factors in complex efforts and in sequences of them."[15] It is through practical experience of sequences of effort changes that a person can determine his own effort make-up and "feel" the effect of certain effort rhythms upon him. In this way he can become conscious of potentials for action of which he was only vaguely aware and so move nearer to an understanding of himself. It is the awareness of this quality which provides us with the dictionary to understand the language of movement.

Without the awareness of effort brought about by effort-training we may develop lop-sided effort responses which are just as restricting as a physical disability. Laban cited the following eight examples[16] of exaggerated effort responses and allied the excessive use of one of the motion factors to behaviour. In these admittedly extreme examples, the continuous use of one factor, in all the actions performed, can, in time, significantly affect the behaviour of a person.

Motion factor	*Exaggerated use of*	*Results (in time) in*
Weight	Strength	Crampedness
	Lightness	Sloppiness
Space	Directness	Obstinacy
	Flexibility	Fussiness
Time	Sustainment	Laziness
	Quickness	Hastiness
Flow	Free flow	Flightiness
	Bound flow	Stickiness

Through effort-training a person can develop the ability to select the most appropriate effort to fit the present situation, for not all movement is apposite. Man finds himself in such a variety of situations in which movement is required and often has no control over the situation but must respond to it as it develops. Thus a stereotyped movement response, whether primarily objective or expressive in intent, is not necessarily the most effective response. Effort-training can provide him with more alternatives for action than those supplied by his natural gifts which are "mostly lop-sided and appropriate to a few tasks only."[17]

Here, I believe, is the core of Laban's belief that through effort-training a person can develop his natural abilities and, through practical experience of effort, be aware of his own responses and the responses of others. Laban believed that "efforts can be transmitted more easily than thoughts"[18] and that it is the effort rhythms of groups of people, whether in the class-room, the football stadium or the religious procession, which creates the atmosphere. On a personal level it is possible, by observing a person's deportment, to see signs of a struggle going on within him. It is not possible to know at once against what he is struggling "though we can learn more if we observe subjective movements—that is, those which do not deal with objects and have therefore no outer cause for struggle."[19] It is these "subjective movements," often very small, which display a person's attitudes to the four motion factors and which, to the skilled observer, can be so illuminating and informative.

Effort-training, and indeed every other aspect of Laban's work, occurs within the *sphere of movement*,

> ". . . the circumference of which can be reached with outstretched limbs without changing one's stance. The imaginary inner wall of this sphere can be touched by hands and feet, and all points of it can be reached."[20]

This sphere of movement has three axes, each one of which is at right angles to the other two. If these axes are assumed to have the same length the resultant solid geometric figure is an octahedron but it is usually represented and referred to as a cube. If this imaginary geometric form in which we stand is related to the space enclosed by it

"... we can discern the three-dimensional cross, which radiates from the centre to the central points of the surface of the cube. The corner-points of the cube are connected by diagonals. Around each diagonal are three diametrals (an intermediate stage between a dimension and a diagonal)[21] and each diametral lies between two diagonals, their outer terminal point being represented by the bisecting point of the twelve edges of the cube. All these twenty-six space-directions radiate from the space-centre, which is the twenty-seventh point of orientation"[22] (*see* Fig. 5).

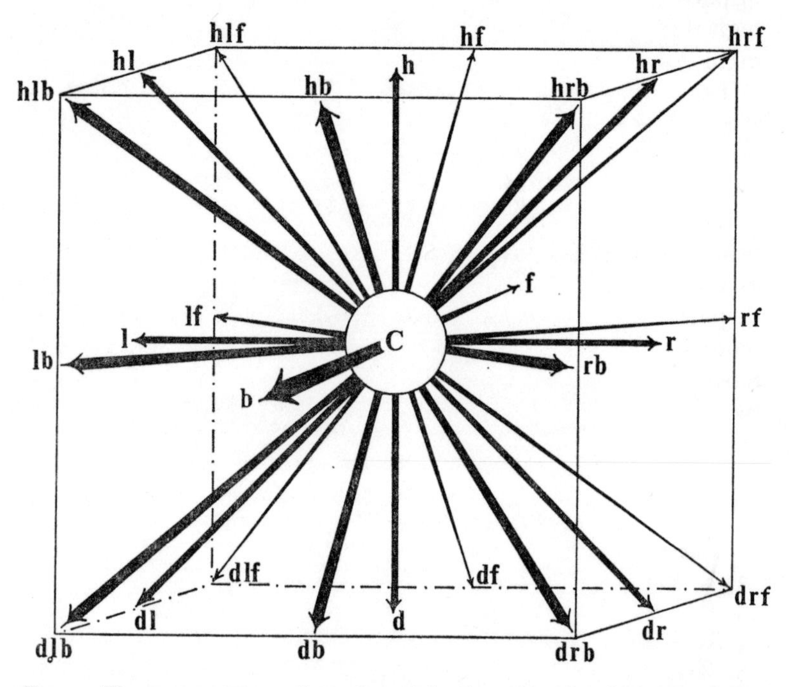

FIG. 5. The twenty-seven points of spatial orientation. h = high; d = deep; l = left; r = right; b = backward; f = forward; c = centre.

The degree to which the space, within the sphere of movement, can be explored is circumscribed by the limitations of the body. Thus the use of this space, by stretching the body to the limits, provides a means of mastering the body in a large number of different situations. There exists, between some of the points in this space cube, quite definite relationships[23] and when specific patterns are being described a particular emotional response is evoked. This response is not aimed at, but is brought about by, the harmony, or disharmony, of that particular space scale or space study. Such space studies can provide the technique on which the expressive side of movement is based. It is also through such training that a thorough understanding of effort is arrived at. Each person has a number of efforts, the demonstration of which comes easily or naturally to him. Each effort uses space in a particular way and there is a direction in which it is most natural for each effort to be displayed. It is not until a thorough knowledge of effort, and a high degree of mastery of the body, has been achieved that a highly defined and selective act of expression is possible.

Thus the basis of Laban's work is an assessment of man as he is revealed through movement. If movement experience is to be of benefit to man it has to make possible self-recognition of individuality, development of potential and a satisfactory way of coming to terms with limitations, and all within a practical situation. This is possible through an awareness of effort which, as has already been stated, involves mental and physical participation and is always displayed in space. Laban develops the relationship between the spatial pattern and the dynamics of movement in *Choreutics*, underlining the importance of these two facets as well as their inseparability.

REFERENCES

1. *Laban Art of Movement Guild Magazine*, November 1957, p. 6.
2. R. Laban: *The Mastery of Movement on the Stage*, p. 2.
3. R. Laban and F. C. Lawrence: *Effort*, p. 1.
4. R. Laban: *The Mastery of Movement on the Stage*, p. 120.
5. *Ibid.*, p. 120.
6. For the arguments expressed in this paragraph I am indebted to Dr. M. G. Mason.
7. R. Laban: *Modern Educational Dance*, p. 8.
8. R. Laban and F. C. Lawrence: *Effort*, p. 58.
9. *Ibid.*, p. 56.
10. *Ibid.*, p. 56.
11. *Ibid.*, p. 56.
12. *Ibid.*, p. 26.
13. *Ibid.*, p. xii.
14. *Ibid.*, p. xii.
15. *Ibid.*, p. 18.
16. *Ibid.*, pp. 37–38.

17. *Ibid.*, p. 18.
18. *Ibid.*, p. 66.
19. *Ibid.*, p. 54.
20. R. Laban: *Modern Educational Dance*, p. 83.
21. *Ibid.*, p. 85.
22. *Ibid.*, pp. 85–86.
23. *Ibid.*, pp. 86–94.

Chapter 5

Principles of Education

Laban's principles of movement encompass his assessment of man and his principles of education may be said to underpin the way in which movement can be used to assist man's development. In Britain Laban's theories have been most widely applied within schools and colleges and many claims have been made for his work, its impact on education in general and physical education in particular. Most of these claims have been made by others than Laban, some of whom were involved in education and could speak with some authority on the application of Laban's theories to the education of the child. Laban did not regard himself as an expert on education; he made statements of educational worth but never appeared to formulate a theory of education. From his writings it would be possible to construct a vast hypothetical formulation of Laban's educational theory but in my opinion this is undesirable. There is, however, a good case for mentioning his educational thoughts and a brief examination of what inferences can legitimately be drawn. *Modern Educational Dance*, Laban's first book on dance directly concerned with education, contained the following statement:

> "Faced with the task of describing the application of the new dance-forms to contemporary school education, the author has had to rely upon the reports of his eminent pupils in this field. His thanks are due to so many of them that they can only be expressed generally.
>
> Due acknowledgment has, however, to be given to those who helped this publication immediately. Miss Lisa Ullmann contributed notes concerning her widespread activity in British schools and teacher-training. Miss Veronica Tyndale Biscoe helped me to make the text as reasonable as possible.
>
> The publication has been urged by the directors of the *Modern Dance Holiday Courses*, who contributed so much to the spreading of the new dance-form in this country.
>
> The conviction that, at an age when the child's natural urge

to dance has sufficiently developed, it is possible and of educational value to base dance tuition upon the principles of contemporary movement research might justify the hope that, with this guide, a useful tool, or at least some stimulus, will be given to educationists and parents interested in the subject."[1]

It was only in Laban's later years that he began directly to apply his theories to the teaching of children, even though from the outset he had been concerned with the growth and development of man, both of which involve an educative process. From his principal works, from his conversations with friends and his lectures, there emerges an implied philosophy of education.

Laban's work in the teaching of children is based upon his work in industry and the theatre. The former gave him the opportunity to analyse movement; the latter to interpret the imaginative world. The observation of movement in industry began during the period 1905 to 1910 when he moved around Europe and the Near East with his father. He was given opportunity to intensify this study during his production of the pageants in Vienna and Mannheim in 1929. The success of his earlier movement observation undoubtedly formed the basis of the application of his theories, in connection with Lawrence, to industry during the Second World War.

Laban's work in the theatre began in his student days in Paris, and his career in the theatre was at its height during the 1920s and early 1930s. At this time there were numerous Laban schools, which were primarily concerned with the training of professional dancers throughout Europe, and Laban was director of movement at the Allied State Theatres in Berlin. His work in England in this field seems to have been restricted to that with the Theatre School and the Children's Theatre in Bradford.

As Laban's studies are concerned essentially with people in learning situations, whether in industry or the theatre, and as in addition be produced an educational manifesto in 1914, his experience of education could be said to have begun at the very outset of his career. He must have influenced many young people, in many walks of life, but it was not until the foundation of the Art of Movement Studio in Manchester, in 1946, that he came into prolonged contact with people who were, during their professional careers, to be primarily concerned with the education of children and adults.

During his life Laban published ten books, only four of which are in English.[2] His works in German are highly complex and demand a specialist knowledge of movement before translation can be attempted. His five works in English reflect fields of study with which Laban was concerned for most of his life. *Effort* (1947) was written as a result of his work in industry with Lawrence; *Modern Educational Dance* (1948) was published two years after the Art of Movement Studio was founded in Manchester; *The Mastery of Movement on the Stage* (1950) is concerned with the application of his theories to theatrical performances; *Principles of Dance and Movement Notation* followed in 1954[3] and *Choreutics*, published in 1966, deals with the understanding and technique of movement with particular emphasis on spatial knowledge.

Effort is based on Laban's movement observation and his analysis of movement by which any movement can be related to the four motion factors. The book is primarily concerned with man at work and with how man and society can benefit from this knowledge which can be brought about by "*selection* and *instruction*. Selection means the putting of the right man on the right job; instruction is the teaching of people how to use the bodily engine in the right way."[4] Both selection and instruction depend on an extensive knowledge of the relationship between the motion factors and effort control. Therefore a programme of effort observation, training, effort utilisation and effort control would benefit both the individual and society.

> "The control of individual effort advocated in this book, and the realisation that this control is based on the observation of rhythmic movement, is not a specific that will cure all evils. Yet, it is a serviceable basis on which to make our selections and examinations, our education and training, and finally also some of our most important social measures and economic decisions, and that in a more humane and adequate way than in the past."[5]

Modern Educational Dance can be described as a guide to those who are engaged in the teaching of movement to children. It is a technical handbook on the logical presentation of movement material, the end product of which is dance. Laban says, "In summarising it can be said that the educative value of dance is twofold: first, through the healthy mastery of movement, and secondly, by the enhancement of personal and social harmony promoted by exact effort observation."[6] Physical mastery of the body can be achieved in ways other than dancing, as can personal and social harmony, but it is only through dancing that these two aims can be achieved simultaneously. Dance can be described as a total immersion in the flow of movement, which is the link between the covert and overt behaviour of man, translating as it does the covert effort life into visible or observable signs. The need to experience this "responds to an urge which all children and many adults feel. The urge to dance, to which all children without exception are subjected from time to time is ineradicable."[7]

While the material and methods by which one assesses children's mental and physical development, as two separate aspects of personality, are well selected, "in the important field of the acquisition of action and effort habits by dancing no reliable selection is made."[8] If a child is to develop his effort-life through participation in dance the teacher needs help to assess the content of this dance experience on the child. The young child needs a consistently widening dance experience if varied effort habits are to be developed. Such development should not be left to the personal taste of the teacher; neither should it be dominated by the popularity of certain dance forms, nor by reminders of the past which are largely irrelevant to the child of today.

It is the task of the properly trained teacher to find those dance movements which "offer the possibility of balancing discordant attitudes and of promoting a healthy growth of personality."[9] This can be done only by a study "based on a thorough knowledge of man's effort-life,"[10] which is dependent on a thorough knowledge and observation of the four visible "factors" of movement. From such observation the teacher, through a movement theme,

> ". . . will learn that a specific movement may have each time a similar impact on the child's mental and bodily attitude. Once a teacher has recognised such facts and collected a sufficient number of examples, the composition of such movement themes as are likely to further the child's development can be undertaken. To do this in a conscious and considerate manner is an art in itself, which can be learnt only through long practice.

This is the way that dance has been used for educational purposes throughout the whole history of mankind. Our time, however, has to find its own procedure, which must take into account the complex form of our present-day education and the whole trend of our modern civilisation."[11]

In *The Mastery of Movement on the Stage* Laban is not concerned solely with dance in the theatre but with every sort of theatrical performance. The basis of any dramatic situation is conflict and the most frequent event which involves conflict is work. By working, man attempts to ensure the necessities of life and in order to do so Laban argues that man is in conflict with his surroundings, his fellow man, his own instincts, capacities and moods.

"But man has added to the struggle with his surroundings, the struggle for moral and spiritual values. The theatre is the forum wherein the striving within the world for human values is represented in art form. . . . The flow of life does not always allow us to contemplate the origin and the consequence of all our acts. We are therefore grateful to the dramatist and to the actors who mirror these happenings for us."[12]

The main source of man's dramatic behaviour is the richness of his effort-possibilities[13] and during a theatrical performance he shows his inner attitudes of mind by a careful selection of efforts, and the conflicts arising therefrom.[14] This depends upon the ability and training of the actor or dancer to recognise his own and other people's movement make-up, which is directly related to the way in which the motion factors are used.[15] Actors, dancers and authors who really know themselves should be fitted to contribute to the true work of the theatre which by its very nature, Laban points out, is a mirror, and not an institution for moral judgment.

"The value of the theatre consists not in proclaiming rules for human behaviour but in its ability to awaken, through this mirroring of life, personal responsibility and freedom of action.

Our present form of civilisation has perhaps greater need than any earlier one to awaken the appreciation of values. The speed of modern life is not only little adapted to quiet contemplation but the feeling after values seems to be steadily atrophying. Many of the old institutions that endeavoured to enshrine moral values in civil and ecclesiastical law are decried, and the individual is left more and more to himself to make his own inner decisions, and to work out the development of his personal responsibility, all of which, of course, is to be deplored."[16]

Choreutics, Laban's last published work on movement, is the most difficult of his books in English. It is the most exhaustive and most technical study of the moving body in space which has yet been produced. Although it is full of diagrams and notation symbols, it is not simply a technical handbook to be used to achieve a more complete mastery of the body. Laban defined choreutics as "the art, or the science, dealing with the analysis and synthesis of movement"[17] which "embraces the various applications of movement to work, education and art, as well as to regenerative processes in the widest sense."[18]

Every movement has a shape and the pathways tracing these shapes in space Laban termed "trace-forms." Some of these will be easily transmutable into other trace-forms and so the movement will flow naturally and organically. Others will need to be stopped or broken before another trace-form can be attempted, thus giving an interrupted or discontinuous quality to the movement. As a person performs a series of actions, the trace-forms of his actions describe a succession of dynamic pathways through space. Even though the dynamic stresses of these pathways

> ". . . are secondary in respect of their spatial visibility they may be regarded as the primary factor in the actual generating of our movements; that is, the generating of visible spatial unfoldings and definite directional sequences with which they form a unity. In reality they are entirely inseparable from each other. It is only the amazing number of possible combinations which, in order to comprehend them, makes it necessary for us to look at them from two distinct angles, namely that of form and that of dynamic stress.[19] . . . To unveil these hidden relations is one of the aims of the study of choreutics and the art of movement."[20]

In a lecture entitled "Education through the Arts"[21] we see Laban's obvious involvement with education. Life, according to Laban, consists of two aspects: the practical world in which a person is concerned essentially with achieving material ends, and that which is not concerned with material well-being, which Laban termed the "dream life" of man.

> "The dream side of human nature has very much fallen into disrepute. It is also assumed that the human capacity of becoming

conscious of the dream side of our life inevitably leads to some irrational mysticism, which cannot be really mastered and controlled.

Exactly the opposite is, however, the case. Our so-called rational behaviours, and the cleverness acquired and upheld with such enormous effort and superstitious lop-sidedness, becomes helpless and hopeless, if its counterpart—the dream life of man—is neglected and almost dreaded. We lose, through such neglect, the control of our life and fall into a state of insecurity which is difficult to remedy."[22]

It is through art that man can boldly and consciously approach his dream life. "Thus we have constantly to feel what we cogitate about, in the same way as we have to cogitate about what we are feeling. Education through the Arts leads to this united and balanced process of living."[23] Through this balanced mode of living man can attempt to find his unity with nature[24] and achieve self-realisation.

It has already been stated that Laban did not appear to formulate a theory of education, yet by a careful analysis of his works in English there emerge four quite distinct educational aims which may be summarised as follows:

Awareness
The creation of situations both at work and leisure in which a person can fully realise his own capabilities and make the most of them. The basis of such self-awareness is a realisation of personal effort characteristics.

Understanding
To attempt to help a person towards a more accurate assessment of himself and, through this, a better understanding of others. The theatre, since it can present both the origins and the consequences of actions and because of the intimacy and immediacy of the situation, has a unique opportunity to awaken a sense of personal responsibility.

Communication
Through this understanding Laban hoped a greater facility for forming good human relationships would be possible, based on the expression of common ideals. Modern educational dance shows a way of preserving and developing man's basic form of

communication through dance. It is hoped that dance experience, which depends on an understanding of effort, would enable a person to be more responsive to the non-verbal communication of others.

Appreciation

That each person, through a heightened appreciation of the form and dynamics of movement, would be more sensitive to shape and rhythms in the natural world; could create and appreciate a wholesome environment in which to live, and would be able to exist harmoniously within his society.

REFERENCES

1. R. Laban: *Modern Educational Dance*, pp. vi–vii.
2. Laban's book *Choreutics*, annotated and edited by Lisa Ullmann, published posthumously.
3. This book is concerned with an explanation of Laban's movement notation.
4. R. Laban and F. C. Lawrence: *Effort*, p. 1.
5. *Ibid.*, p. xii.
6. R. Laban: *Modern Educational Dance*, p. 102.
7. *Ibid.*, p. 103.
8. *Ibid.*, p. 103.
9. *Ibid.*, p. 103.
10. *Ibid.*, p. 103.
11. *Ibid.*, p. 104.
12. R. Laban: *The Mastery of Movement on the Stage*, pp. 104–108.
13. *Ibid.*, p. 14.
14. *Ibid.*, p. 15.
15. *Ibid.*, p. 100.
16. *Ibid.*, pp. 110–111.
17. R. Laban: *Choreutics*, p. 8.
18. *Ibid.*, p. 8.
19. *Ibid.*, p. 36.
20. *Ibid.*, p. 35.
21. *Laban Art of Movement Guild Magazine*, November 1957, p. 5.
22. *Ibid.*, p. 5.
23. *Ibid.*, p. 5.
24. *Ibid.*, p. 6.

Chapter 6

Movement Notation

The contribution of Rudolf Laban to our present and continued research into human movement is freely acknowledged by many people. Any attempt to view this contribution in its true perspective would be impossible without an appreciation of *Kinetography Laban.* Other systems of movement notation have existed, do exist and new ones will probably be developed but, in the view of many, kinetography is the best system to date. There are now available excellent publications[1] which set out the symbols and mechanics of kinetography for the student, so that it is the author's intention only to outline the mechanics of using kinetography. Expertise in the subject will follow from careful study of kinetograms in the recognised standard works and from training with those who are acknowledged experts in the field. Rather is it his desire to outline the reasons for the development of the system and, since movement is the substance of life, emphasise the need for such an ability in all serious students of movement.

The search for a movement notation has persisted for hundreds of years and "when, ages ago, mankind awoke to the idea of standardising pictures and signs in order to communicate certain ideas to one another, bodily actions and gestures were of course included from the very beginning. Early forms of writing are full of signs or symbols for action and movement. No form of writing could possibly omit the enormous number of verbs which, to a great extent, are always bodily actions involving movement. In my search for primary action signs, I found fascinating examples of movement description in the mantic symbols invented by ancient Tibetan monks and in the cuneiform characters of the Assyrians and Babylonians. In Egyptian and Chinese scripts I found a rich variety of movement symbols which are, in a sense, the archetypes of dance notation signs."[2]

The early attempts to notate movement may well have kept step with the development of dance within society and thus the early systems of notation were essentially designed to record and preserve particular movement patterns and not any form of movement. As dance styles changed the system of notation became obsolete and, in most cases, fell into disuse. The movement of the human body exists in space as well as in time and is not a series of single actions but combinations of simultaneous movements. It is not surprising that the early attempts accurately to record complicated dance movements in a legible and economical form and keep abreast with innovations proved so difficult. The earliest known attempt to accomplish this dates from the latter half of the fifteenth century.

Many devices have been tried in an attempt to notate dance. The names of particular steps have been abbreviated; "written descriptions of positions and steps were accompanied by drawings and then given names";[3] the step patterns of the dancer have been written down; "matchstick men" drawings have been combined with musical notes and systems were developed which were based on musical notes. All such systems were only concerned with the presentation, or preservation, of a particular dance style and to endure they would have needed to be more flexible and able to record the movement of the whole body and not just set, static positions and definite step patterns. The system of movement notation as developed by Rudolf Laban "records in vividly legible form all possible movements of the body in space and time (and in a dimension heretofore unattempted—dynamics); it overcomes the obstacles which had impeded progress of all earlier systems."[4] (For an example of Laban's system, *see* Fig. 6.[5]

The study of dance had always been an important feature of Laban's work:

> "Man aspires to be something greater than he is, and knows that he can acquire the greatness that he covets, if only during the imaginative moments when he is lifted above himself in dance. Whether the sincere repetition of such dances produces deeper effects than this, and whether man's spirit is really strengthened by the decision to become his own better self, is an open question. I think we may learn more about this over the years, if we accustom ourselves to notating and pondering the structure of human movements."[6]

Kinetography is thus a logical development of Laban's belief in the significance of movement and dance in the life of man.

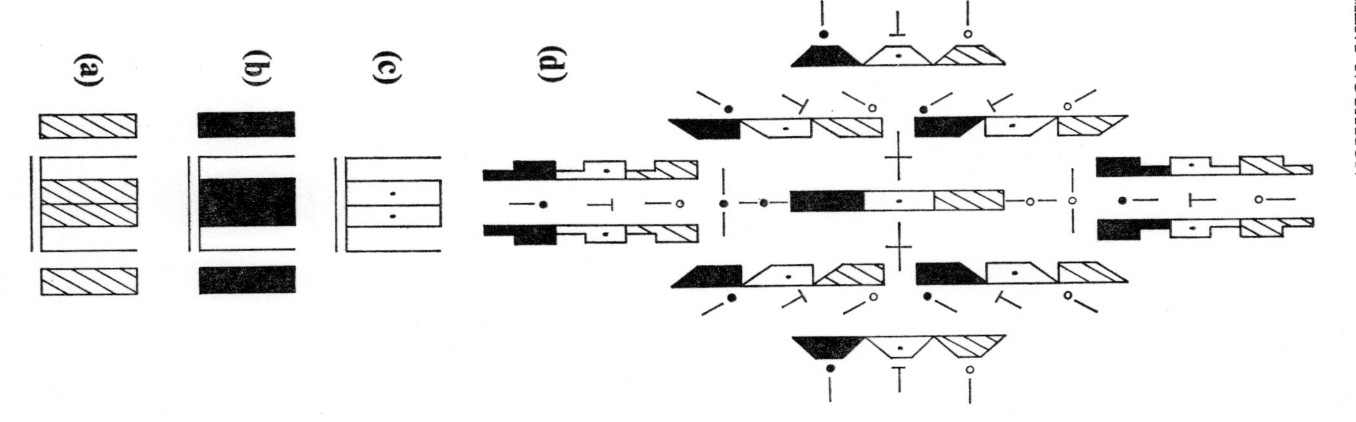

FIG. 6. The notation of weight level and the directions of movement.

(*a*) "This shading of the block-sign by strokes means a *high* level. The example shows: Standing elevated on the balls of the feet, with straight knees. Both arms are raised high."

(*b*) "Shading by blackening the whole block means *deep* level. The example shows: Standing on the whole feet with lowered (bent) knees. Both arms are directed downwards by the sides of the body."

(*c*) "Shading with a dot in the centre of the block means *medium* level. The example shows: Standing on the whole feet with straight knees."

(*d*) ". . . two sets of directional signs are shown."

The larger shaded blocks, of different shapes, can be drawn longer or shorter according to the varying durations of the movements represented by them.

The smaller, pin-shaped signs point to definite directions but have no time value and remain, therefore, always of the same size."

To be able to ponder on the structure of human movements demands a form of notation and Laban's first experiments with movement notation appear to have begun during his student days in Paris. These early experiments were mainly for his own benefit and were no more than "a few meaningful scribbles"[7] but from such beginnings kinetography was developed. This was because "a new and generally acceptable dance notation comparable with the phonetic alphabet had to be built up"[8] in order to preserve and develop man's heritage of dance. Laban acknowledges the help of his pupils and assistants[9] and eminent artists amongst whom were Diaghileff, Toscanini and Siegfried Wagner, all of whom have in their own way contributed to the development of, or encouraged the use of, kinetography. He also expressed gratitude "to our enemies, who have involuntarily helped to overcome the initial weaknesses of the great vision of a literature of movement and dance, with its own language and its own symbolic representation of an important manifestation of the human spirit."[10]

> "Movement notation is a guide to the performance of definite movements depicted in a series of graphic symbols. The writing and reading of notation necessitates an exact knowledge of the signs by which the details of the flow of movement in the body are indicated."[11]

Just as language can be written down phonetically so movement can be recorded graphically.

> "Block-signs, which have been developed from broadened duration strokes, are compound signs containing combined indications of the level, the direction and the duration of a movement. They are called motion characters (the letters of the language of movement). Written into the various columns of the staves, they indicate complex movement actions for each part of the body."[12]

Kinetography contains four of the graphical principles of Beauchamp and Feuillet's system of dance notation:[13]

> "(*a*) The central line separating movements of the right side of the body from those of the left.
>
> (*b*) The partitioning of this middle line by bar strokes indicating a metrical division of time.
>
> (*c*) The use of directional signs and shape symbols guiding the dancer or moving person in space.
>
> (*d*) The indication of basic body actions, such as gliding, hitting, etc., by special stress signs."[14]

Kinetography was conceived so that more than the simple mechanics and timing of dance movements could be recorded.

"It is true that one has to show in a notated dance which part of the body has been moved and its position after it has moved. It is also true that the precise time taken for each movement has to be recorded. But all this must be done in such a way that the essential feature of a dance, namely its flow of movement, is described in all its details."[15]

This flow of movement can be felt in the whole body, or in one or more parts simultaneously, through general or localised muscular activity. The expressiveness of movement depends not so much upon isolated actions but upon simultaneous and sequential combinations of movement. Within such combinations any single movement can be divested of its conventional significance and given meanings which cannot easily be translated into simple words; "For the language of movement consists only to a very small extent of conventional signs replacing, as it were, words and phrases. The main bulk of movement and dance expression consists of motor elements, which can be freely combined to reveal something about the inner state of the moving person."[16] The kinetogram provides a way of recording not only each single action but also its context within the flow of movement and represents, in orthographic form, the moving person's use of the motor elements of Weight, Space, Time and Flow.

In dancing the shapes and rhythms made by the dancer's body convey the "counterplay of definite mental states of balance and harmony . . . a skilled reader of movement notation can not only understand what the body of the dancer does, but shudder or smile on deciphering the mental and emotional contents of the symbols."[17] Any method of recording and preserving this link between inner activity and visible action would seem to have value and possibilities beyond the field of dance. Wherever movement is integral to, or the end product of, human activity a method of notating it would seem of paramount importance.

"The necessity for an adequate script is more urgent now than it was because movement study has come to be recognised as a most important feature in industry, education and therapy. In all three fields a rich tradition of movement knowledge is running to waste, since many bodily actions and exercises cannot be preserved."[18]

It is difficult to over-emphasise the importance of movement notation in any field of movement study. Properly recorded and widely used, it is more than the literature of man's bodily activity. Laban's effort notation provides a way of comprehending the inner life of man through his overt actions. Its basic orthographic shape stems from the time when Laban was, as he says,

> ". . . inclined to condense simultaneous bodily actions around a nucleus having the form of a cross. It is perhaps interesting to mention that this cross became later the basic symbol of my effort notation developed for the recording of body actions in industrial operations connected with the notation of psychosomatic states and inner attitudes."[19]

Laban's method of notation, both the symbols and the manner in which they are written, has remained unaltered since he arrived at its final form. Additions there have been, simplifications also, but the basic structure is intact, proving that the system is sound and practical. Later developments were a source of pride for him too.

> "Quite a large number of people have specialised in the work of notating dances, exercises and movements of artistic, educational, industrial and therapeutic nature, and by the practice of this new profession have added a goodly store of knowledge and experience to my first experiments. The third fact, for which I am even more grateful than I am justly proud, is that I have lived to see several excellent dance creations of our time preserved for coming generations by being written down in my notation."[20]

The uses of kinetography can be as numerous as man's use of movement. In America, due largely to the work of Ann Hutchinson and the Dance Notation Bureau of New York, the system called Labanotation has been most particularly applied to stage dancing. The standard works by Albrecht Knust and Ann Hutchinson show very clearly that kinetography can record any movement and its use need not be restricted to the notation of dances. Valerie Preston-Dunlop, who has an international reputation as a notator, has very clearly illustrated both the flexibility of Laban's original system and its conceptual

LABANOTATION

DANCE OF THE LITTLE SWANS—Balanchine $3.50
BETTER DANCING WITH FRED ASTAIRE—
Astaire studios $3.50
16 DANCES IN 16 RHYTHMS—Shawn $3.50
PLAYTIME IN SONG—Pitcher $3.50
MUSIC FOR THE BALLET CLASS—Keuter $2.50
PRIMER FOR DANCE Bk 1—Hutchinson $2.50
PRIMER FOR DANCE Bk 2—Hutchinson $2.50
THREE R's FOR DANCING Bk 1—Chilkovsky $2.00
THREE R's FOR DANCING Bk 2—Chilkovsky $2.00
THREE R's FOR DANCING Bk 3—Chilkovsky $2.00
SHORT MODERN DANCES—Chilkovsky $2.00
BUTTERFLY ETUDE—Bowman $2.00
THE TEDDY BEARS' PICNIC—Hallenbeck $2.00
THE LITTLE RAG DOLL—Hallenbeck $2.00
DANCING ON MY TOES—Hallenbeck $2.00
AMERICAN BANDSTAND DANCES—
Chilkovsky $1.95
MY FIRST DANCE BOOK—Chilkovsky $1.75
10 FOLK DANCES IN LABANOTATION—
Venable-Berk $1.50
LABANOTATION (cut out) SYMBOLS—Set 1 $1.50
LABANOTATION (cut out) SYMBOLS—Set 2 $1.50
MINER'S DANCE—Hugo $1.25
THREE PRAYERS—Shawn $1.00
DANCER'S GLANCER $1.00
HANDBOOK OF KINETOGRAPHY LABAN—
Knust $10.00
THE MASTERY OF MOVEMENT ON THE STAGE—
Laban $7.50
PRINCIPLES OF DANCE AND MOVEMENT
NOTATION—Laban $4.25
LABANOTATION—Hutchinson $3.50
EFFORT—Laban & Lawrence $3.00
MODERN EDUCATIONAL DANCE—Laban $2.50
MODERN DANCE IN EDUCATION—Russell $2.50

Fig. 7. Modified copy of advertisement in *Dance Magazine* dated August 1961. This indicates the widespread use of Labanotation in America.

soundness through her development of *motif writing*. Motif writing, in which only the outline of a motif is written on a simplified staff, has made the ability to record the essentials of a movement sequence more readily available to those who require such a skill. It may be of interest to note that Laban felt that "very often it is not necessary to notate all the effects of movements contributing to a final effect."[21]

Posture and Gesture by Warren Lamb shows how "details of physical behaviour can usefully be analysed and recorded—in a notation invented for the purpose by Rudolf Laban."[22] Posture is defined as "action involving a continuous adjustment of every part of the body with consistency in the process of variation. Gesture: action confined to a part or parts of the body."[23] Shape and effort are the criteria by which physical behaviour is recorded and assessed. The shape of the body is governed by whether it moves across the vertical, horizontal or sagittal planes and if it grows or shrinks during such movement. Lamb does not use Laban's terms of Space, Force and Time in relation to effort. He finds that they "are a little unfortunate because they invite philosophical speculation"[24] and prefers Indirecting and Directing in relation to Space; Diminishing Pressure and Increasing Pressure in connection with Force, and Decelerating and Accelerating as time indices. His fourth effort category is concerned with the "freeing" or "binding" of the flow of effort. "The freeing effort is of the nature of indulging, yielding, surrendering. . . . The binding effort is of the nature of attacking, contending, controlling."[25]

After observation it is possible to ascertain which of the planes of movement and which efforts are most frequently used by a person and Lamb has developed a form of analysis

> ". . . using a set of observations which can be relied upon as a sample of the subject's physical behaviour. A valid sample for this purpose must consist of at least four hundred phrases equally distributed between the four categories of Posture/Shape, Posture/Effort, Gesture/Shape, Gesture/Effort."[26]

In any sample observation it is not the position which is important but the effort and shape variations which were used to achieve the position which need to be recorded.

Fundamental to the whole process is the desire "simply to

observe physical phenomena for themselves alone"[27] and the principal aim of Warren Lamb's book is to stimulate the ability to observe the physical behaviour of other people.

> "The discovery of the features which are always present in physical behaviour is significant, but it must be interpreted with care. We are not saying that individuals always behave the same in all situations. We are saying that however differently they behave, there are certain features common to their physical behaviour."[28]

With training it is possible to develop a

> ". . . greater range of significant movement. . . . By 'significant' is meant that movement which is an integral expression of your personality (and which can be isolated by analysis) as distinct from movement which consists of habits or mannerisms which have been assumed and which restrict exploitation of the significant movement."[29]

Movement which is, in personality terms, significant can be used as a means of assessing aptitude. Lamb "gives a special meaning to the term Aptitude which is in conflict with some uses of the word. It is here taken to mean a facility for adaptation to a situation which is independent of requirements of technical competence or skill."[30] In Lamb's experience it is possible to help a person more easily meet the demands made upon him by undertaking courses in physical behaviour. Such courses help extend the possible range of posture and gesture variations and have an integrating effect on the personality. Lamb is not alone in this belief, nor in his contention that

> ". . . we are all participants in Dance and Music when we break into expressive movement or into song (or whistling). In most people the former is much more prevalent than the latter.
>
> The idea that dance is or should be a part of life is shared by poets, body-culture experts and a great many educationalists, many of whom are likely to have different ideas on how it should be brought about. It is fundamental to the purpose of this book. It appears also to have dominated the life work of the man whom we can claim, on the evidence of the breadth of his study and extent of his influence, to be the foremost contemporary investigator of physical behaviour. This is Rudolf Laban."[31]

REFERENCES

1. V. Preston-Dunlop: *Practical Kinetography Laban* and *Readers in Kinetography Laban.*
2. Ann Hutchinson: *Labanotation*, Foreword.
3. *Ibid.*, p. 2.
4. *Ibid.*, p. 4.
5. R. Laban: *Principles of Dance and Movement Notation*, p. 32.
6. *Ibid.*, pp. 15–16.
7. *Ibid.*, p. 11.
8. *Ibid.*, p. 13.
9. Jooss, Knust, Hutchinson, Ullmann, Preston-Dunlop, Leeder.
10. R. Laban: *Principles of Dance and Movement Notation*, p. 9.
11. *Ibid.*, p. 21.
12. *Ibid.*, p. 32.
13. Beauchamp's rights as inventor of his dance notation were recognised by an Act of the French parliament in 1666. Feuillet published dances written in this notation around 1700.
14. R. Laban: *Principles of Dance and Movement Notation*, p. 7.
15. *Ibid.*, p. 13.
16. *Ibid.*, p. 14.
17. *Ibid.*, p. 17.
18. *Ibid.*, p. 14.
19. *Ibid.*, p. 8.
20. *Ibid.*, p. 11.
21. *Ibid.*, p. 23.
22. W. Lamb: *Posture and Gesture*, Dust-jacket notes.
23. *Ibid.*, p. 16.
24. *Ibid.*, p. 61.
25. *Ibid.*, p. 56.
26. *Ibid.*, p. 65.
27. *Ibid.*, p. 9.
28. *Ibid.*, p. 154.
29. *Ibid.*, p. 177.
30. *Ibid.*, p. 154.
31. *Ibid.*, p. 88.

Chapter 7

The Development of Movement in Education

In schools and training colleges the work of Rudolf Laban has been applied in three fields: (1) dance, (2) drama, (3) physical education; and an attempt will be made to see how they embrace the aims of education which are implied in Laban's writings. Each one of these three aspects of the art of movement provides opportunity for a child to realise his own capabilities and exploit them. Each is important in its own distinctive way in the education of the child, offering various paths for self-exploration. Physical education allows the child to experiment with his bodily skills and experience conflict in a socially acceptable and patently obvious situation. By the width of the field that it covers physical education also can provide a great deal of satisfaction for a great number of children. Dance and drama, although concerned with the body, are dependent upon a knowledge of effort and through this an understanding of human personality. Dance, drama and physical education all hope to further the formation of good human relationships by offering children different methods of communication with one another. Dance and drama, together with other forms of art, can provide opportunity for the child to integrate his physical, mental and spiritual qualities into one act of "creation."

Such an act is unique, for it can never be exactly repeated as it arises out of a singular situation which is appertaining at that point in time. Just as the situation is inimitable, so also are the attitudes and emotions of the participants. In drama this can occur when children start with an idea for a play, write their own script, make their own costumes, scenery and properties and finally put on a full-scale performance. It may also happen within one single lesson when a dramatic situation is improvised with each child taking a full part in the improvisation. In dance a child may choreograph a dance for himself, or combine with others to produce a dance for a small or large group. When such dances are performed solely for the benefit of the dancers, each child has an opportunity to contribute something from within himself and it is hoped that, through this, a feeling of oneness with the cosmos will be felt—a rare experience.

Valuable though such experience may be, Laban's view is that a study of the art of movement is not exhausted by studying movement from just these three aspects. He is quite definite about this, for he said:

> "The creative type of modern educational dance originating from the practice of the art of movement is represented in, or adapted by, Physical Education in a very fragmentary way only.
>
> Neither of the border subjects of physical and mental [drama] training in the forms cultivated in the schools of our day is able to fulfil the essential task of real action training."[1]

Here is a plea for the art of movement to be studied as a course in its own right and it is a point of view accepted, to some degree, by many colleges of education who offer main dance courses and courses concerned with the art and science of human movement. However, until movement courses become completely independent, branching out to the various aspects of the subject from the central focus, we cannot significantly progress from our present knowledge and understanding.

Movement may become a term to cover dance on the one hand and physical skills on the other. Movement is a characteristic of human life and, as such, would seem to demand continued investigation, so that the particular opportunities it offers are utilised to the full.

> "The whole subject, in its central position between Physical Education and Language Education, and with its relation to music, art and other subjects, offers more than one chance to help in the development of the personality of all children, to the greatest possible extent of their natural gifts."[2]

The fact that children can now participate in creative dance situations in schools, that there is generally much more movement awareness throughout education, and that dance courses continue to develop throughout the country is largely attributable to the spread of Laban's ideas. This has been accomplished in the face of considerable opposition and not without controversy and, even though Laban was resident in England before the outbreak of the Second World War, the impact of his work in education was not felt until some considerable time after hostilities had ceased. The war had cut the teacher-training programme and the whole of the education system was working under a pressure which was not beneficial to the spread of new ideas. The people who attended the courses organised by Laban during the 1940s did not have facilities, in the schools, which were conducive to a rapid spread of his work.

It would be difficult to attempt an accurate assessment of the situation in education, and particularly physical education, in those early post-war years. The war undoubtedly caused re-examination of many previously held positions and attitudes in physical education. However, some convictions survived this period of evaluation for they reappear in books written after 1945. The historical development of physical education is beyond the scope of this work, yet some examination of the practice of physical education around the late 1940s and early 1950s is required if the influence of Laban is to be appreciated. It is only possible to attempt this review by referring to books which were used by teachers and thus deduce the movement experience of children, the way in which specialist teachers were trained, and the emphasis and standards which were set in both schools and colleges.

In November 1954 a reprint of the London County Council's *Syllabus of Physical Training for Boys in Secondary Schools*[3] contained a paragraph which could be regarded as a summary of the sort of movement experience which was regarded as normal for that time.

> "It will be noticed that these tables contain both free-standing exercises and exercises which require portable apparatus. Those teachers who are qualified to use apparatus, and whose schools are thus equipped, will be able to employ the whole range of movements outlined in these tables. If apparatus is not available, or if the teacher is not qualified to handle this type of work, then only the free-standing exercises, jumps, simple agilities and games should be attempted."[4]

It is recognised that this publication would be directly influential only in London schools but I feel sure that many copies of it were used outside of the London service. The London County Council felt that a daily period of physical activity was to be aimed at in all its schools and of these "an allowance of three periods weekly to physical exercises, one to swimming and one to organised games, will often be found suitable."[5]

An examination of the tables shows that the exercises are grouped under anatomical headings.

> "The more formal exercises of the first section of the lesson should still be commanded but not necessarily counted or synchronised. . . . The teacher should start each movement with a direction and give an indication when each exercise should stop. Whilst the movement is in progress he should be observing carefully, encouraging and coaching for good performance either on the part of the class as a whole or those boys who need special help. His attention should, therefore, be focused on the essentials of good movement and not on the less important fact of class synchronisation."[6]

The second part of each of the tables is devoted to skill development under headings of ball handling and the major national team games and athletics in the outdoor situation; indoors it is devoted to climbing, balancing, vaulting and agilities and minor games. The Council believed that "physical education embraces all types of physical activity and the aim should be to produce all-round skill"[7] and that there was equal merit in producing a skilled athlete, gymnast or footballer. To help teachers to develop both the gymnastic and non-gymnastic aspects of physical activity the second half of the book is devoted to agilities, vaults and various games.

Books which were published between the years 1948 and 1954 conformed fairly generally to this pattern and were supported by specialist publications which dealt with a particular aspect in a more detailed and comprehensive way. The movement experience of secondary school boys was thus devoted to the acquisition of skill across a whole range of physical activities, yet within each of these different situations the goal for *every* child was quite clearly defined. If this was true in schools it was also true in men's specialist colleges where a typical week for a student would be a daily session of gymnastics, one or two hours per week spent in the swimming bath and one or two afternoons spent on the games field. Lectures on anatomy and physiology, the history of physical education, the theory of gymnastics, the major team games and the place, aims and objectives of physical education would complete his timetable. By the late 1940s women's specialist colleges included dance in their programme but, at the majority of colleges, dance was no more important than gymnastics, games or swimming.

Without doubt the emphasis was very firmly placed, both in specialist colleges and schools, on personal performance, especially gymnastic performance. Students who were proficient at gymnastics were assumed to have something the athlete, swimmer or games player did not have and this "halo" effect was carried over to their teaching ability. If the same criterion had not been carried into schools, the London County Council would not have seen the necessity of commenting that "the physical-training lesson has been viewed by many members of the profession as a means of producing gymnastic skill rather than skill in all types of physical activity."[8] Marshall and Major had made the same sort of plea in their book, in 1940, but their recommendation "that in every physical training lesson there should be included a variety of recreative activities designed to provide pleasurable activity for all the children and not merely for those who are good at vaulting and agility exercises"[9] seems to have gone unheeded for at least fourteen years.

The other standard by which the effectiveness of a physical education programme was judged, at least at a school level, was posture. In 1932 this statement appeared in *The Health of the School Child*, which was the annual report of the Chief Medical Officer of the Board of Education.

> "If there is one test of the strength, tone and balance of the body it is posture, for this depends on the co-ordination of the muscles acting on the skeleton. Good posture indicates health and soundness, bad posture the reverse."[10]

The physical education profession had shown an interest in remedial work for many years and remedials and correct posture training are but two shades of the same colour—the therapeutic nature of gymnastics. This link with the medical profession goes back to the 1920s and was still apparent in 1954. "Training for good posture and carriage is therefore a matter of first importance during the secondary school period and should not be confined to the physical training lesson only."[11] The approach to physical education in the primary school, even before the war, was much less formal than in the secondary school but even the 1933 Syllabus maintained that "emphasis is laid upon good posture, both in rest and in action."[12]

The years between publication of the 1933 Syllabus and the next official Ministry publication in 1952 saw a reappraisal of the State education system. It was during these years that Laban arrived in England and the Art of Movement Studio was established in Manchester; it is beyond question that Laban's ideas were contributory to *Moving and Growing.*[13] This book could be regarded as giving Ministry approval to child-orientated physical activity which emphasised self-expression, movement awareness and the importance of dance in primary schools. At this time at secondary level, the practice of physical education had been widened to include all sorts of activities, in- and out-of-doors, of a recreative or competitive nature. The indoor lesson included "besides attention to vaulting and agility, coaching in the skills fundamental to a wide range of games and athletics."[14] The desire to construct tables of exercises "not so much upon the basis of exercising each and every part of the body as upon the effect that the exercises should have upon these parts"[15] led to re-examination of formal gymnastics. The make-up of the new tables, divided as they were into a "mobilising section, a strengthening section and a skill-learning section,"[16] seems to have been more a difference in method than a new concept, since the emphasis was still upon the training and coaching of good performance.

The Second World War disrupted the educational and social systems of most European countries and opened the door for the re-examination of basic values. Such a period of re-examination is conducive to the adoption and development of new ideas, and the spread of Laban's work was undoubtedly helped by this fluid situation. I doubt whether movement education would be what it is today had not Laban's ideas and work been well established in England. I do not mean to imply that without Laban there would have been no development in physical education, but I do maintain that Laban's influence on the physical activity of all children in school has been as significant as that of any other single person since the Second World War.

REFERENCES

1. *Laban Art of Movement Guild Magazine*, March 1952, p. 12.
2. *Ibid.*, p. 16.
3. Inner London Education Authority, County Hall, London, S.E.1.
4. London County Council: *Syllabus of Physical Training for Boys in Secondary Schools*, p. 5.
5. *Ibid.*, p. 5.
6. *Ibid.*, p. 16.
7. *Ibid.*, p. 89.
8. *Ibid.*, p. 89.
9. F. J. C. Marshall and E. Major: *A Book of Physical Education Tables*, p. 10.
10. P. C. McIntosh: *Physical Education in England since 1800*, p. 204 (cites Annual Reports of the Chief Medical Officer, 1932, p. 81).
11. London County Council, *op. cit.*, p. 13.
12. Board of Education: *Syllabus of Physical Training for Schools*, 1933, p. 7.
13. Ministry of Education, H.M. Stationery Office, London, 1952.
14. M. W. Randall: *Modern Ideas on Physical Education*, p. 15.
15. P. C. McIntosh, *op. cit.*, p. 239.
16. *Ibid.*, p. 239.

Chapter 8

The Controversy over the Spread of Laban's Ideas

To people interested in physical education the name of Rudolf Laban is synonymous with movement. Movement usually means controversy. This controversy may be concerned with: whether gymnastics and dance are part of the same field of experience; the relationship between the art of movement and the acquisition of specific sporting skills or whether Laban's terminology can be applied to all branches of physical activity. That there has been considerable disagreement is some indication of the impact of Laban's work. Some have welcomed Laban's theories as a completely new concept of physical education and have applied them to all branches of the subject. Others have rejected them completely and there are many degrees of acceptance and rejection between these two extremes.

The *Journal of Physical Education* has, in some of its articles, reflected various shades of opinion about movement. Such articles give a more accurate picture of the attitude of the physical education profession as a whole than reference to the Laban Art of Movement Guild magazines.

The first Ministry-aided course at the Art of Movement Studio was begun in September 1949, so the first Studio-trained teachers left Manchester around the middle of 1950. The way in which these students were trained was probably very similar to that outlined in an article in the *Journal*.[1] The contributors to this article were the lecturers on the staff at the Studio and so it was able, within the space available, to give a comprehensive picture of the work at Addlestone. In this article the position of dance, in the training of the students, is fairly closely defined.

> "The integration of emotional feeling and mental control at which the training mainly aims makes it understandable how vital the practice of the art of movement is in education. Enlightened educationists and authorities in many parts of the world have supported the idea of introducing what is frequently called 'modern educational dance' in schools. This form of dance

tuition is one of the branches of the art of movement. . . . Our work at the Studio does not only serve the simple release of bodily energy, but has a deeper aim and effect. Reconciliation of the so-often divergent, emotional and mental trends within a personality is achieved through the study and practice of the art of movement. . . . The student must become aware of his movements. He must appreciate his bodily, spatial and rhythmic capacities before he can use them to the full and realise his limitations before he can begin to enlarge his range. . . . In dancing, the student will be aware in an intuitive rather than an intellectual way of the significance of the experiences made in moving. In the study of movement an effort is made to enrich and balance the personality, by advancing the knowledge of the inner resources of man. . . . Education through movement is not limited to the dance class."[2]

While the training of these students was directed primarily towards dance, they, in conjunction with the teachers of physical education who had attended Laban's summer schools, had begun to make an impact on teachers of physical education. An article appeared in the July 1951 number entitled "The Old and the New in Physical Education." This article saw the new approach as something which stressed

". . . the individual child in the physical education lesson, with emphasis on the unfolding of the inherent possibilities for movement in the individual—a 'creative' approach to the lesson in which the child is encouraged to express his own movements, in his own way, guided by the teacher."[3]

However, the cult of the individual must not be pursued too vigorously:

". . . it may simply lead to selfishness and waywardness. What is essential is that the child should express himself in patterns which are socially acceptable. Better still, for full development of his total person, his motor activities should involve him to a greater or lesser degree, dependent upon his level of maturity, in pleasurable association with other members of his group."[4]

It would seem that while it is permissible to develop the individual this must be done within some structure which is easily recognisable, the value of which is practically universally accepted, in short, team games. It is possible that the new approach was seen as a direct threat to everything which was an established fact in physical education. This was not the intention, for the fundamental principles behind Laban's work complement physical education. I feel sure that these principles, if applied on a purely physical level, are aimed at getting the most from the human body in terms of body awareness and body management. They are not envisaged as the one process by which the skills appropriate to a particular sport are more easily learned.

"Another introduction is an aspect of our work labelled Modern Dance with an aesthetic and emotional content that is new to our accepted pattern" comments the *Journal.*[5] The word "emotional" has overtones which imply unstable behaviour. Any aspect of physical education containing an emotional content would, through lack of definition of this word, appear to be in conflict with the accepted tradition of the "stiff upper lip."

> "The 'old' way did not stray very far from the purely physical in the gymnastic lesson. Children did work which became progressively stronger and acquired certain principles about movement and the use of apparatus. The 'new' way attempts far more in introducing both an emotional and dramatic aspect into a lesson which previously followed a very limited pattern."[6]

If creative movement—used in the way in which Laban understood it—was introduced in the gymnastic lesson, then the plea to stop and consider whether in older children "the desire for self-expression may by now have found other channels than those of physical education"[7] was quite justified. Others saw the "new" approach as a combination of the new trend in educational thought, the influence of modern dance and Austrian gymnastics.[8] While dance and the modern gymnastic approach both recognised the need to allow scope for individual "creation," "in the gymnasium especially, the teacher should keep a clear picture of the physical side of the training and the qualities which may be stimulated by his teaching as well as allowing scope for creation."[9] This would suggest that the work in the gymnasium was becoming more concerned with the subjective, to the neglect of the objective, side of physical education. The influence, from whatever source, which finally resulted in the sweeping away of the pre-war concept of the physical education lesson was something to be welcomed even though at this time the concept of the physical education lesson would appear to have gone from one extreme to the other.

Even though T. Poppe considered that the "new" approach involved children in a situation which was educationally more valid than before (because "it is the experience of the pattern of movement . . . which gets across to the child, releases him and makes him receptive for our educative work"),[10] the introduction of this dramatic and emotional element, to the possible exclusion of skill learning, was not welcomed by everyone. It was inaccurate

> ". . . to think that those of us who have used Laban's principles of movement in dance work, for some time, also welcome their present influence on women's gymnastics, and are convinced of their total effectiveness. While Movement Training may be useful in facilitating the later learning of skills, can it really take the place of a systematic instruction in techniques? . . . Surely it is possible to study a middle course here, and while accepting in general the value of Time, Strength and Space as factors of movement, to acknowledge the necessity for a narrower path of approach at a certain point in skill learning."[11]

Here is a request to select from the art of movement those aspects which are appropriate to gymnastics.

This controversy had been going on for at least two years and it was not until 1955, in the July issue of the *Journal*, that a definite statement was made about the "middle course" for which Miss Roberts had pleaded. On the assumption that gymnastic apparatus limits movement and therefore movement experience, "the full range of movement experience is only possible when one is free of apparatus and this kind of movement leads naturally to expressive dance. Expressive movement is out of place in the gymnasium where the whole situation is objective."[12] This opinion, so clearly stated, does not split objective and subjective movement into two separate subjects. It simply advocates putting the child into situations which are essentially subjective or objective, for in either case he is studying a branch of the art of movement.

In 1961 an article appeared in the *Journal* in which the distinction between gymnastics and dance was redefined.

> "In gymnastics the concern is with functional movement, with body management and with mastery of the body in tackling the

> challenge of the apparatus. In dance the concern is with expressive movement, with mastery of the body to use the language of movement creatively."[13]

A thorough understanding of the art of movement could help the teacher to prevent a gymnastic lesson from becoming a succession of "favourite movements" on the part of the child. Such tendencies have to be guarded against if any progress in self-exploration is to be made.

A. D. Munrow examined the question of whether the physical training involved in a study of the art of movement would contribute to an all-round general ability in the performance of specific skills. In his article[14] he quotes from page 9 of *Modern Educational Dance*, on which the following reference to games is made

> "Games imply the knowledge and experience of the movements used in them, which requires a technique of moving. This technique, like that used in the skilled performance of industrial operations, is a part of the art of movement."

In view of this and other statements of a similar nature, Munrow came to the following conclusion:

> ". . . by a sound grounding in certain fundamental types of movement . . . one can prepare the ground, so to speak, for the superposition of the particular skills which require the particular movements. I will not question the transference of this sort of training."[15]

The statement from *Modern Educational Dance* is certainly worth a close examination, for while it only mentioned games it can surely be applied to every other pursuit of skill in the physical educational programme. The acquisition of particular skills is necessary if activities demanding these skills are to be subsequently undertaken. As these skills are highly specialised they require a detailed and quite specific study. Such a study is part of the art of movement. The impact of Laban's ideas on gymnastics has come about through the way in which the child has been given opportunity for personal exploration in relation to apparatus. On this premise skill patterns should be encouraged which are of the child's own choosing, and he should not be constantly directed towards some predetermined gymnastic goal. However, the traditional vaults should not be ignored, for they demand a degree of co-ordination, strength and courage which is of a very high standard.

An article in the *Journal* in 1953 illustrated the extent to which movement training had spread throughout some branches of physical education. Movement training was being applied in situations which were, to some people, inappropriate.

> "By restricting the older girl to the Movement Training approach to specific skills, we are denying her the benefit of systematic instruction based on the accumulated experience of generations . . . in general the effective application of the principles of Movement Training for specific skills seems to me to be an over-ambitious claim."[16]

In view of Laban's statement, to which reference has already been made, it would be interesting to know who was making such claims. Laban never did. Here is a case of the over-enthusiastic, indiscriminate application of a sound principle to every situation, however inappropriate such an application might be. These inadvisable excursions into the world of skill learning, no matter how well intentioned, could well have misrepresented the true value of movement training, and therefore movement.

While A. D. Munrow had accepted that the body awareness, on a purely physical level, brought about by movement training, was a basis on which it was possible to build a whole series of specific skills, he did not say that it was the only way, or the best way. Laban never suggested that a thorough physical training in the art of movement would automatically mean that specific skills would be learned more readily. Marjorie Randall thought that Laban believed particular skills would be more easily acquired through a movement approach than by a more traditional method. She took up this theme of movement training in relation to specific skills in March 1956.

> "People trained in the eight basic actions combined with bound and fluent flow will be more able to choose the appropriate movements for any tasks they face than those who rely entirely upon their natural gifts or intuition."[17]

This statement means, surely, that a person who has had some form of general physical training will be more able to select a movement appropriate to a new situation than someone who has had no training at all. However, Randall drew the following conclusion:

> "So presumably Basic Movement should be a foundation for all physical skills. But no experimental evidence is offered to support this claim which is at variance with the general trend of informed psychological opinion. It follows, then, if Laban's statement be true, that a Basic Movement approach should result in a skill attainment in hockey, swimming, vaulting, etc., higher than if these skills had been more directly approached by more traditional methods."[18]

This is a startling deduction, especially in view of Laban's statement, "Training for a definite task will best be done on the object during operation."[19]

In this same article Miss Randall also raised the question of the terminology evolved by Laban.

> "The ensuing discussion at Liverpool made it evident that both dancers and gymnasts prefer to interpret with different shades of meaning and words some of Laban's phraseology. This would suggest that though highly desirable, a common language of Kinaesthesis has not been generally accepted."[20]

Some women's colleges of physical education used Time, Weight, Space and Flow in the teaching of "water skills, diving and lacrosse."[21] Presumably it is the dynamics of movement with which Miss Randall is concerned, for Laban had published a book on movement notation some two years prior to the article by Randall. It must be admitted that "the choice of words for dynamics has been, and still is, a stumbling-block for people who are not thoroughly familiar with the effort graph"[22] and, while it is possible to analyse movement in terms of Weight, Space, Time and Flow and describe movement by use of the eight basic efforts, Laban pointed out that these verbal terms were not adequate for the full description of movement.[23] It is very difficult to verbalise all human experience and action; if it were possible to do this there would be no music and no art. Music has its own set of symbols which are used to transmit its meaning or feeling, yet we still persist in our attempt to codify, classify and describe movement in words, a medium which is usually hopelessly inadequate for this purpose.

Since the beginning of the 1960s there has not been an

article in the *Journal* which could be regarded as "controversial." Physical education is developing new approaches, particularly with reference to the indoor lesson and games, at both secondary and primary level and these developments may well have brought about a more accurate understanding of the role of dance and physical education in education. Dance has now established itself as a depth study in Britain, yet it appears to incur inert or passive opposition within some Institutes of Education who refuse to offer a student the option of taking a Bachelor of Education degree in dance. Even those Institutes which have such a degree insist upon such an emphasis on written work that, to the uninitiated, dance would seem to be a purely intellectual activity.

If it is believed that practical work is imperative, and that it illuminates, clarifies and demonstrates, in patently visible terms, a grasp of the theory, then the emphasis should be placed where it belongs, on the ability of the student to work with and through dance. If an examination of dance is required, and this includes written work, then the examination should be made to meet the dynamics of the subject and the subject should not be trimmed to meet the requirements of an Institute of Education. It is the task of those colleges of education which hold this view to persist in their endeavours to have their views accepted by the academic hierarchy, no matter how much conflict this may provoke.

Dance has aroused much controversy, even to reach its present state of acceptance, so how much more controversial would be the establishment of the study of the art of movement, in Laban's terms. To date there are only two places in England which provide the opportunity to study movement in a context broader than dance. These are the Art of Movement Studio in Addlestone and the Beechmont Movement Study Centre in Sevenoaks. The cost of running private ventures is enormous and how long the former can survive official pressure to be even more closely integrated into the education system and the latter withstand the withholding of official recognition is, unfortunately, open to speculation. It is only through education that society can be made aware of the values of movement understanding and it is not until the universities and the Department of Education and Science will accept that "education through movement is not limited to the dance class"[24] that movement study will become significant and achieve its full potential in the education of man.

REFERENCES

1. *Journal of the Physical Education Association*, March 1954, pp. 23–29.
2. *Ibid.*, pp. 23–29.
3. W. L. Steel: *Journal of the Physical Education Association*, July 1951, p. 42.
4. *Ibid.*, p. 44.
5. *Ibid.*, p. 42.
6. E. Karn: *Journal of the Physical Education Association*, July 1952, p. 65.
7. J. O'Dwyer: *Journal of the Physical Education Association*, July 1951, p. 46.
8. R. Clark: *Journal of the Physical Education Association*, November 1951, p. 130.
9. *Ibid.*, p. 130.
10. T. Poppe: *Journal of the Physical Education Association*, July 1953, p. 62.
11. C. Roberts: *Journal of the Physical Education Association*, November 1953, pp. 93–96.
12. V. Sherborne: *Journal of the Physical Education Association*, July 1955, p. 48.
13. J. Russell: *Journal of the Physical Education Association*, November 1961, p. 83.
14. A. D. Munrow: *Journal of the Physical Education Association*, July 1952, p. 52.
15. *Ibid.*, p. 52.
16. C. Roberts: *Journal of the Physical Education Association*, November 1953, p. 94.
17. M. Randall: *Journal of the Physical Education Association*, March, 1956, p. 15 (cites Laban: *Effort*, p. 18).
18. *Ibid.*, p. 15.
19. R. Laban and F. C. Lawrence: *Effort*, p. 18.
20. M. Randall, *op. cit.*, p. 17.
21. C. M. Webster: *Journal of the Physical Education Association*, November 1958, p. 86.
22. V. Preston-Dunlop: *Journal of the Physical Education Association*, July 1967, p. 51.
23. R. Laban and F. C. Lawrence, *op. cit.*, p. 26.
24. *Journal of the Physical Education Association*, March 1954, p. 29.

Chapter 9

Books Influenced by Laban's Theories

Most of the authors who have written on the subject of movement within the sphere of education admit to the influence of Rudolf Laban. Some, however, would have us believe that their work arose spontaneously, implying that they have never been affected by a book on movement. All their books were published after 1945, with the exception of one by Diana Jordan which was published in 1938, the year that Laban came to England. This work, *The Dance as Education*, is worth study for if reference had been made to one of the few people in England who had ever attended a Laban school, some of the controversy which raged in the late 1940s and early 1950s might well have been avoided.

In the interest of clarity the books will be dealt with in four sections—those which are:

1. specific to dance,
2. dual purpose (dance and gymnastics),
3. specific to gymnastics,
4. specific to games.

(Only one volume can really be classified under the last category.)

They will be examined to see whether they are concerned with the same deduced educational aims as Laban, which were: awareness, understanding, communication and appreciation. (*see* pp. 57–58). It will be interesting to see whether they contain any extension of Laban's thought or ideas as expressed in his works.

1. Books which are specific to dance

By 1939 dance (and this included country, national, folk and some expressive dance) had been recognised as a significant part of the physical education programme. This recognition, which was most helpful in those early days, could be the reason why teachers of physical education still regard dance (in its new context) as part of their responsibility. "In many schools, dance is only a physical education, at its best a series of exercises to the accompaniment of music, at its worst a superimposed form of expression exercised within a strict formula and set to music to which it is totally unrelated."[1]

To Diana Jordan, dance was more than mere physical education; it was something which involved the "whole person" and which did not really come within the jurisdiction of the physical education specialist. "To begin this understanding of 'Dance,' we must first place dance in the school, not as a part of physical training, but as one of the arts."[2] This view may be more acceptable now than it was at the time when this book was published. Dance, as defined by both Laban and Jordan, is chiefly concerned with the individual in a variety of situations, for the following reason.

> "Just as there are no two minds alike, so there are no two people who move naturally in precisely the same way, partly as a result of different personality, partly as a result of unique physical structure; therefore, if we are to assist the co-operation of mind and body, it is the harmony between a particular mind and a particular body that we seek to achieve, and not that between a standardised body and mind."[3]

So in dance the individual has to be made aware of what he is, and what he can do well, and this is particularly important while the child is in school, for school presents an environment which is designed to allow children to realise their abilities and fulfil them. The same thing cannot be said of the world at large.

Books written on dance, after the publication of Laban's works, assume a knowledge of the subject and they are therefore primarily concerned with the practical application of Laban's theories. The first of such books to appear was *Modern Dance in Education* (1958) by Joan Russell. In this the theme of awareness is taken up under "the all-round development of personality." This she believes, like Bruce, is brought about by personal experience of effort-training, which is designed to make a person aware of himself, for "the effort actions are ways in which the human person moves when the inner attitude demands such effort."[4] The assumption is made that movement is not mere motion. If this assumption is accepted as correct, then it must be realised that "the individual expresses his inner attitude and intention through his movements, so conversely we believe that, by introducing the person to a richer and more varied movement experience, we can enrich his inner experiences."[5] By so doing[6] we make him more aware of himself and his potential.

From self-awareness it is possible for the individual to develop deep understanding of his fellows. Interpretation of another's behaviour and personality is attempted by everyone.

> "As we go about our daily activities we use our powers of observation to assess a person's general attitude, or mood of the moment, and use this knowledge to adjust our attitude to him. Someone sits screwing a handkerchief into a ball and we note nervousness; we receive a vigorous slap on the back from a hearty friend; a child stamps his feet in a temper-tantrum. From such observations we learn something of the person."[7]

The basis for these observations is our own movement experience and this includes not only movements we make but movement we observe. "We live in an environment full of movement. It is a manifestation of life itself and one way in which we can learn to understand the world is through our sense of touch and movement."[8]

> "In dance we should instinctively react to one another and create situations for one another which have to be dealt with, as much as we do in life. . . . This requires quick and sympathetic reaction, spontaneity, adjustment and judgment . . . which is required of us in everyday life if we are to be fully aware of each other's needs without wordy explanation, and which enables us to act, or withold action, to join in, or hold apart, to go with, or to go alone; in a word, to act as constructively as possible, both for ourselves and for a common purpose."[9]

It is by co-operation of this sort, whether with one individual or a group, that the "most basic form of expression can be developed as a prime means of comprehending the common factors in our varied experiences of the environment."[10]

To understand people communication is essential. As the means of communication become more exact it is possible to convey ideas or emotions more accurately. Dance is one medium, other than verbal, which can facilitate communication.

"Dance is a means of unspoken communication that takes place between dancers, between dancers and onlookers, or between dance teacher and pupils. . . . But the fact is that we depend in everyday life, to a larger extent than is often realised, upon the same unspoken communication. Even when struggling for words . . . how often do we feel the emotions of another, or of a crowd, in silence; and how thankful we are for the inestimable value of this unspoken communication when working with people who react instinctively to one another and to what is required."[11]

The joy of a child, "his anger, his sulkiness can all be observed in his posture and gesture";[12] they clearly demonstrate his ability for non-verbal communication. Adults do not normally display their true reactions as readily as a child but it is "the use of this or that part of the body, the distinctive effort quality used, the clarity of the trace-forms in the space, the awareness of the relationships evolved"[13] which show a person's response.

Communication through movement requires a mastery of the body to allow it "to be used expressively in order to serve as a means of communication."[14] Increasing bodily proficiency and sensitivity, which arises from becoming "conscious of the way in which movement takes place and of the qualities involved,"[15] gives the dancer a rich fund of experience upon which he will draw for development of his dance ideas. Mastery of the body does not come without practice and study and such training is part of the art of movement.

Both Jordan and Russell saw dance as a natural method by which man attempts to find his own place in the cosmos, for dance has always been used by man to express his important feelings and needs and "the nearer people live to nature and are affected by its rhythms, the more spontaneous their expression in movement."[16] As man becomes more sophisticated he not only loses his ability to express himself through movement, he begins to lack "experience of the world of movement, of flying through the air, beating fast against the ground, spinning and whirling, carving pathways through the space, moving with care, with abandon, with haste, with leisure, with more tension, with less tension—all this, and more besides, is yet another aspect of the way in which we come to grips with the universe and with the fundamental manifestation of life and living matter which is movement."[17] Dance springs from this fundamental manifestation of life and "involves the whole person in an extraordinarily balanced way . . . no other activity demands so equally the use of the intellect, the body, the emotions and the intuition."[18]

Dance is a language which knows no barriers and by learning "something of the dance styles of other countries and other times the dance language is enriched and some understanding given of other people and cultures."[19] The child is encouraged to retain and develop the ability to become completely involved in movement experience and expression because

> ". . . in so doing, we assist nature's own method of physical education, that is to develop the mind through outside stimulus conveyed via the body and to develop the body through the purposeful action which expresses the mind, for we are not body and mind but mind–body and body–mind and whatever we do with either affects the other."[20]

Three books, by authors who were trained personally by Rudolf Laban, may be called technical handbooks, by which no disrespect is implied. Both authors obviously know a great deal about the theory and practice of teaching dance and the art of movement, and their books must have brought the teaching of this complex subject within the understandable grasp of many teachers. Both assumed that their readers have accepted the value of movement teaching and they do not, therefore, seek to justify its worth. They are concerned with the sixteen movement themes that Laban enumerated in *Modern Educational Dance* and acknowledge that Laban's movement theories are the basis of their work.

In the preface to *A Simple Guide to Movement Teaching* Marion North stated: "Constant reference is made to *Modern Educational Dance* by Rudolf Laban—the book which will give the fundamental principles underlying the work in education."[21]

Valerie Preston (now Valerie Preston-Dunlop), in *A Handbook for Modern Educational Dance*, said:

> "Since they [the sixteen movement themes in *Modern Educational Dance*] were first introduced, teachers have been experimenting with them and the richness inherent in each has gradually unfolded. It is the intention of this book to describe more fully each Theme in the light of the experiments which have been made, and some suggestions as to how they might be used in schools are put forward."[22]

Both these works present the movement themes in a way which gives more help and guidance than did Laban, and Valerie Preston-Dunlop's book, because of the extent and wealth of practical suggestions it contains, would seem to be a necessary companion volume to *Modern Educational Dance.*

In her second book on movement, *Composing Movement Sequences,* Marion North stated:

> "There are two aspects of recreation which have been developed from Laban's work in movement. The first is concerned with the experience gained from movement sequences, simple or complex; the second is the quite different experience of taking part in dance compositions, which have been called 'Movement Choirs' or 'Recreative Dances' . . . This booklet is concerned with the dance composition of movement sequences, which may be dance-like but which are not complete dances."[23]

Introducing Laban Art of Movement by Betty Redfern (1965) is designed to replace a previous Laban Art of Movement Guild publication entitled *The Art of Movement in Education, Work and Recreation* which is now out of print. It contains the general outlines of the specific principles behind movement and is not concerned with the way in which Laban's theories can be applied in school. By enumerating the use of movement in education, industry, therapy, the theatre and in recreation, it shows what a wide field of study is possible within the art of movement.

Creative Dance for Boys by Jean Carroll and Peter Lofthouse is, in essence, a practical handbook on the presentation of material which in their experience is suitable for boys at secondary school. Their initial approach to dance teaching with boys of this age is through hard physical work. Even though they adopt this approach they "do not subscribe to the view that only powerful action is masculine"[24] because "dance is concerned with organising and coming to terms with, expressing and commenting on, human experience."[25] The practical suggestions and the fact that the book has been written may encourage more men to undertake the teaching of dance to boys. That Laban's work is the basis of this book there is no doubt; indeed the authors acknowledge the help of Miss Lisa Ullmann and others who have considerable experience of movement. This volume and Miss Joan Russell's *Creative Dance in the Secondary School* may be regarded as something of a breakthrough, the former since it is concerned with dance for boys, the latter since it deals with dance for older school children.

Throughout Jane Winearls' book *Modern Dance: The Jooss–Leeder Method* constant reference is made to the "basic principles of the dynamic order and design harmony of movement"[26] which Rudolf Laban had published in his book *Choreographie* in 1926. It should be remembered that at that time Laban was primarily concerned with dance in the theatre and the training of dancers for the theatre. Thus as well as giving rise to modern educational dance Laban's work has made a fundamental contribution to a particular professional dance style.

In Jane Winearls' opinion Laban's contribution to dance is not limited to the Jooss–Leeder method, for "the greater part of Modern Dance development in Europe (in America it started from a different appraisal of the laws of physical movement) grows logically and quite consistently from Rudolf Laban's work as a movement-experimenter. Beginning with the work of Delsarte, of many kinds of folk dance, of the laws of mathematics and geometry, he evolved a means of 'dissecting out' the basic elements which *create and control* every kind of movement of which the human anatomy is capable. His work was furthered by the collaboration of Kurt Jooss and Sigurd Leeder, who, starting with the methods and experiments promoted by Laban, carried movement research further until there was evolved the Jooss–Leeder method whereby the dancers of the Ballets Jooss were trained. The importance of this company for over a quarter of a century in the field of modern dance is an indication of the value of this method."[27]

The purpose of Jane Winearls' book is to provide both the teacher and the student of dance with a handbook of practical suggestions related to the Jooss–Leeder style of dancing. Her attitude was as follows:

> "Between Educational Modern Dance and the American Modern Dance of the entertainment world, there is room for an artistic whole which can link the classroom with the stage and educate the person whilst training the dancer. . . . The Jooss–Leeder Method has been taught all over the world, and has helped to bridge the gap between dance as an educational activity, and dance as a fully matured art of the Theatre."[28]

Her book is also intended to "preserve, in its technical form, the joint work of Kurt Jooss and Sigurd Leeder, who have developed this method from the inspiration and fundamentals of Rudolf Laban."[29]

The books in this section all follow the educational principles of Laban. Preston, North, Carroll and Lofthouse use Laban's basic movement themes as the basis of their work, and as these are the vehicle through which Laban's educational principles are effected, they therefore adhere most accurately to his educational precepts. By the same token they cannot, therefore, offer any philosophical extensions to his work. Jordan's book, written as it was as long ago as 1938, cannot be expected to contain any progression of Laban's thoughts, for it preceded Laban's own publications in English. Nevertheless, it does embrace Laban's educational tenets. For the author to have achieved this at that time was a considerable feat, for in those pre-war days Laban and his principal pupils were concerned with training dancers for the stage and not with the education of children. The books of Russell and Bruce use Laban's work as an obvious source material for their own publications. Whilst they do not offer any extensions of his work their books do contain their own significant interpretations of Laban's ideas.

2. Dual-purpose books (dance and gymnastics)

Within this category come the two books issued by the Ministry of Education. While many influences resulted in these Ministry publications, "Laban's ideas were certainly contributory to the publications *Moving and Growing* and *Planning the Programme*."[30] The physical education lesson envisaged in both these works was to contain "abundant opportunity for movement, opportunity to develop skill, a wide field of experience leading to versatility, and the growth of awareness."[31] In an attempt to promote awareness the Ministry shifted the emphasis from the pursuit of skill as the only way in which movement could be used.

> "The pursuit of skill alone is not enough; it may even lead to narrowness and specialisation, neither of which is suited to the needs of growing children. Rather is it desirable to widen the field of their experience so that it is rich and varied, and so that they become expressive as well as dexterous, graceful as well as

strong, agile as well as steady. Children of this age should be able to enjoy their skill in many directions."[32]

In an attempt to promote awareness the Ministry gave many helpful suggestions. The awareness brought about by the use of expressive movement, used in conjunction with objective movement, is regarded by the Ministry as an art. This "implies an attitude to movement which is quite different from our approach to swimming or gymnastics, for example, because we shall be concerned, not with movement as a means of performing some feat, but with its expressive quality."[33] The task of the teacher in dance was to help "the development of the individual movement so that it is rich and varied in quality, to support the gradual growth of the power to develop and sustain ideas, and to encourage, as the children become ready for it, the capacity to work in groups as well as individually."[34] It was hoped, therefore, that group dance would further understanding.

Laban's third educational aim—communication—was also recognised as important by the Ministry, for they stated:

"It seems important that we should help children to enjoy as rich an experience in movement as we do in language, where we try to help them to widen their vocabulary, to use language flexibly, to write and speak expressively. In movement our aims may be described as similar."[35]

Group dance was acknowledged by the Ministry as one way in which it was possible to achieve awareness, understanding and communication. However, as far as I could see, the Ministry did not draw directly on Laban's theories, so, even though his ideas may have influenced the writers of these two books, there is only a tenuous link between Laban and *Moving and Growing* and *Planning the Programme*.

3. Books which are specific to gymnastics

To the majority of young people modern gymnastics is educationally and physically a more satisfying experience than that gained from traditional vaulting and agility. The modern approach could be said to be aimed at developing "an understanding and appreciation of objective movement coupled with the ability to invent and select appropriate actions,"[36] and it could be argued that this aspect of the work, the opportunity for invention and selection, more clearly reflects the influence of Laban's ideas than does the actual content of the lesson. Laban had shown that movement has more than a physical dimension, springs from desires and is aimed at goals at which it is only possible to guess. His analysis has provided a way of understanding movement and, even within the gymnastic lesson, evaluating the potentials and limitations of both the child and the class.

Many authors of books on gymnastics have acknowledged Laban's influence on their work. The present writer will examine these books to discover how Laban's theories have been applied to the gymnastic situation. This process should not be regarded as an attempt to define or justify gymnastics, nor as a critical review of such books. It is rather an attempt to chart the extent of Laban's influence on the movement experience of children. That the emphasis of the gymnastic lesson is now placed where it belongs—upon the child's physical awareness of himself, brought about by his movement experience and his personal response—is, in some measure, attributable to Laban's work.

Gymnastics can offer an unrivalled opportunity in helping a child to become aware of himself, his abilities and in presenting an opportunity to realise whatever abilities he has. The number of combinations and permutations of gymnastic apparatus used in relation to the emphasis on different body shapes, etc., makes it possible to present an ever-changing pattern of purposeful activity. It is hoped that such experience will develop his sense of self-awareness and assist him to an awareness of others. Co-operative gymnastic activity requires an awareness of others, even if only taken at a very simple level. This theme of awareness is taken up by Ruth Morison in her book *Educational Gymnastics* which

> ". . . purposely deals only with the outward and visible actions and omits any mention of the stimuli which cause them or of the attitudes of mind which induce them. For those who want more detail, it is all explained much more fully and profoundly in Mr. Rudolf Laban's book, *Modern Educational Dance*."[37]

Morison illustrated the importance of awareness at a "physical level." "A teacher of movement should take into account all such personal differences, as well as recognising the different ways and rates of learning. The first step is to allow each individual to move in her own way and to help her through this way of moving."[38] The teacher should "value the contribution which each child has to make, not only with physical effort but with thought, imagination, ingenuity, inventive powers and originality. Our task is to help each child to discover and develop her own movement potentials."[39] In Ruth Morison's second book, *Educational Gymnastics for Secondary Schools*, she again stresses the necessity for awareness.

> "Gymnastic skills . . . give the individual mastery over himself in a wide variety of situations. . . . An awareness of the body in movement and a feeling for what different parts of it can do, are also needed to carry out the activities of gymnastics; therefore, activities which develop such awareness should form part of every lesson."[40]

These thoughts are echoed by Marjorie Randall when she writes that " 'body awareness' implies a greater conscious investigation of the feel and balance and control of the body, and thus includes more than was meant by the old terms of 'neuro-muscular control' or 'co-ordination'."[41] Such awareness comes about by a

> ". . . growing understanding and mastery of their bodies in movement and as confidence and sensitivity develop their movements become competent, fluent and skilful. . . . The body is regarded as the agent or instrument of movement. If an instrument is to be well and fully used a knowledge of its parts and its potentialities is necessary. The child therefore should be made aware of one part of the body in relation to other parts or to the whole, and the term 'body awareness' is associated with these experiences."[42]

Furthermore, Cameron and Pleasance comment that:

> "Mobility is maintained, co-ordination is developed and the correct application of strength is encouraged. . . . If we are to justify our work we must avoid a response that fulfils the limitation and yet demands little effort from the child. He should always be striving for form, quality and coherence in his performance. . . . The result of gymnastics taught with these principles in mind is an increased efficiency in the development of the individual's physical ability."[43]

It would seem that awareness is the one educational aim of Laban's work which is most readily applicable to the gymnastic situation. Participation in various partner relationships and co-operative group work are a recurrent feature of modern gymnastics and depend upon each child's appreciation of his own movement and the movement of those with whom he is involved.

There are some authors, however, who make claims for modern gymnastics which go beyond the aim of awareness. They feel that gymnastics, based on the movement approach, has a carry-over value to other aspects of physical education. This is possible because "there is a vocabulary common to all movement so that terms learned in one situation have meaning in another."[44] In Marjorie Randall's view the movement approach is "concerned with an entirely different form of gymnastics, one that is based not upon Ling's classification, not on Munrow's, but upon Laban's movement qualities."[45] Some authors admit that the movement approach "has infused new life into gymnastic skills,"[46] yet maintain that "enthusiasm for such an approach need not—it is here suggested, should not—exclude completely the traditional skills."[47] They also question whether the

> ". . . body awareness achieved through working on Laban's effort qualities and according to his movement principles develops . . . a power of effort selection and appropriate application that is transferable to other fields of skill activity."[48]

It would seem that the controversy which arose from the application of Laban's theories to gymnastics revolves around four points:

1. Traditional versus modern.
2. The carry-over value of gymnastics.
3. The use of Laban's terminology.
4. The presence of a subjective element in some gymnastic work.

The place of the traditional vaults in the gymnastic lesson appears to have resolved itself since the mid 1950s. I think it would be fair to say that the stereotyped responses these vaults require is not now regarded as a sufficiently broad gymnastic experience for all children. The use of Laban's terminology and the transfer of training have already been considered on pages 80 to 82 and so will not be re-examined.

That some authors and teachers had reservations about Laban's work in relation to gymnastics is obvious; otherwise there would have been no controversy. When the validity of the movement approach is examined they question, at least by implication, the value of Laban's work, since those who advocate such an approach quote Laban's books as source material for their claims. It is not usual for authors who quote Laban to give direct references in his books but rather to find a statement such as, "This work is based upon the movement principles of Rudolf Laban. Further clarification of these principles are contained in his books *Modern Educational Dance* and *Effort*." They omit to show the way in which they have simplified or interpreted Laban's ideas. Because Laban's theories are not clearly detailed it is thus often impossible for the reader to do other than totally accept or reject the interpretation and the original theories.

Cameron and Pleasance admit that "some readers will protest that we have over-simplified Laban's *Principles of Movement*, leading thereby to some slight inaccuracies of interpretation. This has been done deliberately so as to avoid confusing those unfamiliar with the terminology of the subject."[49] Since they do not detail Laban's original principle nor their simplification of it, it is possible to deduce that Laban advocated a teaching method and that his motion factors have none other than functional significance. Whilst acknowledging that Laban's "philosophy and analysis of movement are the basis of the modern gymnastic lesson.... In order to stimulate the child to develop his physical powers and abilities, and, at the same time, an understanding of movement, the teacher must have a knowledge of Laban's analysis."[50] Their reduction of this analysis to the how, what and where of movement does less than justice to a system which is focused on *why* a person moves and the significance of such movement.

There still appears to be some confusion and controversy on how far Laban's theories can be applied to gymnastics and Laban himself wrote:

> "Thorough effort-training can be achieved only through dancing, as gymnastics, games, dramatics and art are more

concerned with the result of actions, and not with the action movement itself."[51]

In the opinion of E. Mauldon and J. Layson, authors of *Teaching Gymnastics*, there is still much misunderstanding concerning the place of the four motion factors—Weight, Space, Time and Flow—in gymnastic teaching and physical education. They consider it

> "A disservice to try to remould Laban's ideas or graft them on to well-established physical activities. The motion factors provide a basis for understanding all movement and in Physical Education, with the exception of dance, the stress is on objective function, a part of movement only. Thus it is not a matter of 'applying' Weight, Space, Time and Flow to a particular activity but the reverse, that is, appreciating how the activity can be considered in the light of these fundamental principles."[52]

Gymnastics is an objective situation in which the measurable aspect of Weight, Space, Time and Flow is important.

> "Thus, in referring to the Weight factor in gymnastics, it is the degree of energy and bodily tension that is considered. In Space the gymnast is concerned with direction, level, pathway and body shape, while in Time the degrees of speed provide the content. The relevant aspect of the Flow factor is that of control."[53]

Children take a certain amount of time and expend energy as they control their movement through space but even though the motion factors together are the substance of gymnastics they do not, in isolation "provide gymnastic themes."[54]

In response to any gymnastic task an individual's response will inevitably be coloured by his personal rhythms "which will effect the way of moving but not the end result."[55] The very nature of the objective situation means that "gymnastic actions demand specific effort combinations. Certain proportions of the motion factors are stressed and others, though present, are latent,"[56] yet "the fun of producing something which is 'mine' and the excitement and satisfaction of working with others has an educational value not to be ignored."[57]

4. Books which are specific to games

E. Mauldon and H. B. Redfern, in their book *Games Teaching, A New Approach for the Primary School*, maintain that "the teaching of games continues in the main to be carried along traditional and even stereotyped lines, with few questions asked as to the reason for its inclusion in the curriculum."[58] They question the validity of the reasons usually given for the inclusion of games in the school's time-table. In their experience the socialising and character building associated with games is nothing more than a supposition as is "their usefulness as a compensation for academic studies and as a safety valve for surplus energy and high spirits; their value as a healthy exercise in the open air; and not least their importance as a preparation for the use of leisure in later life. Not one of these, however, is defensible on educational grounds."[59]

The way in which so many young people opt out of games as soon as they are given the opportunity to do so may well have led to the authors' review of the place of games in the primary school.

> "It is not surprising that many young people of today reject outright for very good reasons the image of toughness, heartiness and unquestioned loyalty to a particular group not of their own choosing, which is associated with their experience of games."[60]

It is the authors' intention to justify the teaching of games on grounds which are educationally sound.

> "Unless games can be of educational value for every child they deserve no place in a school time-table (as distinct from after-school-activities), least of all when strong claims for inclusion at Primary level are all the time being successfully pressed by so many other subjects."[61]

The authors felt that the "general area of Primary school Movement Education"[62] was hardly different from that type of games teaching which helped children

> ". . . to find out for themselves, to pose questions, to solve problems, to look for underlying principles and discover how things are related to one another; to use their powers of inventiveness and imagination; to select from a range of possibilites, to assemble, construct and formulate both alone and with others."[63]

Whilst the name Laban is not mentioned in this volume they seem to acknowledge one of the basic tenets of his work in their contention that "the integration of doing, thinking and feeling is becoming recognised as essential to the educative process."[64]

REFERENCES

1. D. Jordan: *The Dance as Education*, p. 2.
2. *Ibid.*, p. 2.
3. *Ibid.*, p. 9.
4. V. Bruce: *Dance and Dance Drama in Education*, p. 18.
5. J. Russell: *Modern Dance in Education*, p. 19.
6. The reader is referred to Laban's first principle.
7. J. Russell, *op. cit.*, p. 18.
8. J. Russell: *Creative Dance in the Primary School*, p. 12.
9. D. Jordan, *op. cit.*, pp. 10–11.
10. J. Russell: *Creative Dance in the Secondary School*, p. 21.
11. D. Jordan, *op. cit.*, pp. 30–31.
12. J. Russell: *Creative Dance in the Primary School*, p. 12.
13. J. Russell: *Creative Dance in the Secondary School*, p. 87.
14. J. Russell: *Modern Dance in Education*, p. 21.
15. V. Bruce, *op. cit.*, p. 34.
16. J. Russell: *Modern Dance in Education*, p. 13.
17. J. Russell: *Creative Dance in the Primary School*, p. 18.
18. J. Russell: *Creative Dance in the Secondary School*, p. 18.
19. V. Bruce, *op. cit.*, p. 29.
20. D. Jordan, *op. cit.*, p. 7.
21. M. North: *A Simple Guide to Movement Teaching*, preface (private publication).
22. V. Preston: *A Handbook for Modern Educational Dance*, p. xiv.
23. M. North: *Composing Movement Sequences*, p. ix (private publication). This work and *A Simple Guide to Movement Teaching* are to be published shortly by Macdonald & Evans under the combined title of *Introduction to Movement Study and Teaching*.
24. J. Carroll and P. Lofthouse: *Creative Dance for Boys*, p. 14.
25. *Ibid.*, p. 10.
26. J. Winearls: *Modern Dance: The Jooss–Leeder Method*, p. 11.
27. *Ibid.*, p. 11.
28. *Ibid.*, p. 15.
29. *Ibid.*, p. 15.
30. Foster: Letter, *see* Appendix II, p. 128.
31. Ministry of Education: *Moving and Growing*, p. 52.
32. *Ibid.*, p. 52.
33. *Ibid.*, p. 60.
34. Ministry of Education: *Planning the Programme*, p. 20.
35. Ministry of Education: *Moving and Growing*, p. 61.
36. E. Mauldon and J. Layson: *Teaching Gymnastics*, p. xii.
37. R. Morison: *Educational Gymnastics*, p. 4 (private publication).
38. *Ibid.*, p. 3.
39. *Ibid.*, p. 4.

40. R. Morison: *Educational Gymnastics for Secondary Schools*, pp. 8–9 (private publication).
41. M. Randall: *Basic Movement*, p. 15.
42. London County Council: *Educational Gymnastics*, p. 2.
43. W. McD. Cameron and P. Pleasance: *Education in Movement*, p. 4.
44. R. Morison: *Educational Gymnastics in Secondary Schools*, p. 7.
45. M. W. Randall: *Basic Movement*, p. 12.
46. M. W. Randall: *Modern Ideas on Physical Education*, p. 127.
47. *Ibid.*, p. 127.
48. *Ibid.*, pp. 124–125.
49. W. McD. Cameron and P. Pleasance, *op. cit.*, p. ix.
50. *Ibid.*, p. 3.
51. R. Laban: *Modern Educational Dance*, p. 24.
52. E. Mauldon and J. Layson, *op. cit.*, p. xii.
53. *Ibid.*, p. xiii.
54. *Ibid.*, p. xiii.
55. *Ibid.*, p. xii.
56. *Ibid.*, p. xii.
57. *Ibid.*, p. xiv.
58. E. Mauldon and H. B. Redfern: *Games Teaching*, p. 1.
59. *Ibid.*, p. 2.
60. *Ibid.*, p. 3.
61. *Ibid.*, p. 5.
62. *Ibid.*, p. 16.
63. *Ibid.*, p. 16.
64. *Ibid.*, p. 16.

Chapter 10

The Increase of Laban's Influence

Laban's ideas and movement principles have influenced many people in the years since the Second World War and the books written on movement and dance indicate to some small degree the extent of this influence. These books can be regarded as the source to which those interested in movement refer for clarification, material or stimulation. The great majority of such people are involved in education and it is in schools and colleges that Laban's work has been most widely used.

In an attempt to chart the extent of Laban's influence within education two questionnaires were sent to colleges of education. The first, sent in 1964, contained questions which related to that year and 1954. The second related only to 1969. It was not intended that the results obtained would be statistically significant, nor will they be interpreted in a way which suggests that the findings are conclusive for the whole country. However, the fifteen years covered by the questionnaires give some indications, in the very broadest terms, of the way movement teaching has developed in colleges.

As both specialist and non-specialist colleges affirmed that their courses in movement were based upon the principles put forward by Rudolf Laban, it would seem that *all* students who follow a movement course in a number of colleges are influenced by Laban's work. No indication of the interpretation of Laban's

TABLE 1

Percentages of staff who taught movement and who had attended the Studio

	1954	**1964**	**1969**
(*a*) *Percentage of total staff who:*			
(i) taught movement	30	30	37
(ii) were women movement teachers	30	24	30
(iii) were men movement teachers	—	6	7
(*b*) *Percentage of movement teaching staff who:*			
(i) had attended the Studio	48	61	53
(ii) were women and had attended the Studio	48	57	38
(iii) were men and had attended the Studio	—	4	15

principles was asked for since it was felt that such a request would have been presumptive and unrealistic.

Information was requested in connection with the numbers of staff who were employed; taught movement; had attended the Art of Movement Studio. From the answers received it is possible to compile the preceding table. It must be re-emphasised that this table is not statistically significant and that the answers are being interpreted in a descriptive manner.

Although incomplete, some interesting indications emerge from this survey:

1. that the percentage of staff employed to teach movement is increasing;
2. that of this percentage the number who have attended the Art of Movement Studio, even though it is decreasing, is still over 50 per cent;
3. that the percentage of women who have attended the Art of Movement Studio is dropping; with regard to college appointments, there is an increased percentage of Studio trained men.

The trends indicated in (1) and (2) can be regarded as inevitable and entirely logical. As main-study movement/dance courses have been established, the products of these colleges must eventually begin to fill at least a reasonable proportion of the posts in colleges. It may well be said that what is happening with regard to women may, as dance becomes more firmly established as a depth study for men, also happen with regard to men in colleges of education.

Within colleges of education a movement/dance course in its own right, as a specialist or non-specialist study, appears to be a comparatively rare occurrence. The vast majority of such courses form part of a physical education programme. Some colleges offer movement/dance as part of a drama course or an "induction" course for all first-year students. All those colleges that study movement to any depth also study a method of movement notation, the most widely used being motif writing.

It can be assumed that a proportion of movement-trained teachers will be concerned with movement in schools. In addition to this direct and personal method there are the B.B.C. movement programmes. Since the B.B.C. transmit

Music and Movement I, *Music and Movement II* and *Music, Movement and Mime* an approach was made to ascertain whether Laban's theories were contributory to the movement content of these three programmes. Vera Gray, who, as well as being the producer, also selects and arranges the music, attended many courses taken by Laban, whilst Rachel Percival, responsible for the movement content of the programmes, was trained by him. However, Vera Gray emphasised that these schools broadcasts were based upon an interpretation, arrived at after consultation with Rachel Percival, of Laban's principles, and were not therefore directly attributable to his work. Despite such a tenuous link between Laban and the B.B.C.'s movement broadcasts I feel that the table below is worthy of consideration.

TABLE 2

Estimated Audiences in Primary Schools: Autumn Term 1968

1. SERIES FOR INFANTS AND LOWER JUNIORS

Series	*Infant schools*	*Jnr. schools without infants*	*Jnr. schools with infants*	*Total schools in target*	*Total*
Music and Movt. II	4,819 (87·4)	2,717 (55·0)	9,891 (73·0)		17,427 (72·7)
Music and Movt. I	5,095 (92·4)	741 (15·0)	11,278 (83·4)	16,373 (86·0)	17,114 (71·4)

2. SERIES FOR JUNIORS

Series	*Jnr. schools without infants*	*Jnr. schools with infants*	*Total no. of jnr. schools*
Music, Movt. and Mime	1,438 (29·1)	3,912 (28·9)	5,350 (29·0)

The figures in brackets express the number of schools following each series as a percentage of the total number of schools of that type in England, Wales and Northern Ireland.

Source—*Facts and Figures*: School Broadcasting Council for the United Kingdom. The Langham, Portland Place, London WIA IAA.

Laban's work focuses primarily on education and this is reflected in the membership of the Laban Art of Movement Guild. The list of individual members and affiliated groups illustrates the international flavour of the Guild and the educational bias which has been given to Laban's work. The Guild provides courses, conferences and one-day study sessions for its members, whilst the Junior Laban Art of Movement Guild or affiliated groups of the Guild promote days of dance for school children. The work of the Guild is not necessarily directed towards the application of Laban's theories to education since it is concerned with movement experience in its broadest context. The Guild is open to anyone who wishes to join, irrespective of previous experience, and it is possible to progress through the different categories of membership without being a teacher.

An article in *The Guardian* draws attention to a further development in the spread of Laban's work in Britain. The Keep Fit Association is "not just a bunch of women waving our arms and moving our legs about" according to its chairman Mrs. Netta Thomas. "The Keep Fit Association has moved on from the old knees-bend-arms-stretch routines to new exercises based on modern educational dance forms, mostly carried out to music or percussion. Weights and waists are no longer the key targets. Neither is mentioned in the latest Keep Fit Association publicity pamphlet. They have been replaced by such goals as poise, grace and the promotion of physical and mental well-being."[1]

If the Keep Fit Association can promote the physical and mental well-being of its members through practical experience of modern educational dance forms then it will have brought experience of Laban's work within the knowledge of a previously untouched percentage of the population. It is hoped that this sort of experience will encourage further and more detailed study, propagate the spread of Laban's work and prevent movement study from becoming an esoteric pursuit in schools and colleges divorced from the world at large.

For some concrete facts on the situation in movement teaching, the following questionnaires were sent to colleges of education offering a "Wing" course in physical education and to those which come within the University of Leeds Institute of Education. Information was requested so that some picture of the development of movement teaching in colleges could be attempted. It was felt that the fifteen years covered by the questionnaires were helpful and adequate in this respect.

Questionnaire 1

1964

1. Name of college

		10 years ago	*Today (1964)*
2. The number of P.E. lecturers on the staff	women		
	men		
3. The number of lecturers in Movement and Dance	women		
	men		
4. The number holding the diploma of the Art of Movement Studio	women		
	men		

	For women	*For men*
5. Is a movement course held:		
(*a*) as part of the P.E. programme,		
(*b*) as part of a drama programme,		
(*c*) as a course in its own right.		

6. (*a*) Does the course extend over three years?
   (*b*) If not, and if not included in (5), do you offer any movement course at all?

7. Would you say that the movement course is based on the principles put forward by Rudolf Laban?

TABLE 3

Question No.	2				3				4				5						6		7
	10 yrs. ago		Today		10 yrs. ago		Today		10 yrs. ago		Today		Women			Men			(a)	(b)	
	W	M	W	M	W	M	W	M	W	M	W	M	(a)	(b)	(c)	(a)	(b)	(c)			
Anstey	7	–	7	–	3	–	4	–	2	–	3	–	Yes	No	Yes	–	–	–	Yes	–	Yes
Avery Hill	4	–	6	2	I	–	2	–	–	–	2	–	Yes	Yes	No	No	No	No	–	–	Yes
Barry[1]	2	–	5	–	I	–	–	–	I	–	–	–	Yes	No	No	No	No	No	–	–	Yes
Bedford[2]	8	–	12	–	6	–	9	–	3	–	6	–	–	–	–	–	–	–	Yes	–	Yes
Bingley[3]	2	–	2	2	2	–	2	I	–	–	–	–	Yes	Yes	Yes	Yes	Yes	Yes	–	–	Yes
Bishop Otter	2½	–	7	I	I	–	2	–	–	–	I	–	Yes	No	Yes	Yes	No	Yes	Yes	–	Yes
Borough Road	–	2	I	3	–	–	–	–	–	–	–	–	Yes	No	No	Yes	No	No	No	–	Yes
Bretton Hall	I	I	2	I	2	–	2	3	–	–	2	–	Yes	Yes	Yes	Yes	Yes	Yes	Yes	–	Yes
Cardiff[4]	–	3	4	8	–	–	2	–	–	–	I	–	Yes	No	No	Yes	No	No	–	–	Yes
Carnegie	–	7	–	14	–	–	–	5	–	–	–	–	No	No	No	Yes	No	No	Yes	–	Yes
Chester	–	I	I	7	–	–	I	–	–	–	–	–	Yes	No	No	No	Yes	No	No	–	Yes
Derby[5]	3	–	5	2	I	–	2	–	–	–	3	–	Yes	No	–	–	–	–	Yes	No	Yes
Endsleigh	I½	–	4	–	I½	–	2	–	–	–	I	–	Yes	No	No	–	–	–	Yes	–	Yes
James Graham[6]	–	–	I½	–	–	–	–	–	–	–	–	–	Yes	Yes	No	Yes	–	No	No	–	Yes
Lady Mabel	4	–	8	–	2	–	4	–	2	–	3	–	Yes	Yes	Yes	–	–	–	Yes	–	Yes
Leeds[7]	5	3	5	3	–	–	–	–	–	–	–	–	Yes	–	–	Yes	–	No	–	–	Yes
I. M. Marsh	3	–	9	I	3	–	5	–	3	–	5	–	Yes	No	No	–	–	–	Yes	–	Yes
Margaret McMillan	–	–	–	2	–	–	–	–	–	–	–	–	Yes	–	–	–	–	–	–	–	Yes
Neville's Cross[8]	I	–	5	I	–	–	2	–	–	–	I	–	Yes	–	–	Yes	–	–	Yes	–	Yes
North Riding	I	I½	–	–	–	–	Non	Full-time	–	–	–	–	Yes	No	No	–	–	–	No	–	Yes
Ripon[9]	I	–	2½	–	–	–			–	–	–	–	Yes	No	Sub-sid	–	–	–	No	–	Yes
																				–	No
St. John's	–	3½	–	6	–	–	–	I	–	–	–	I	No	Yes	Yes	Yes	Yes	Yes	Yes	–	Yes
St. Luke's	–	4	–	9	–	–	–	I	–	–	–	I	–	–	–	Yes	Yes	No	No	–	Yes
St. Mary's[10]	–	I	–	5	–	–	–	–	–	–	–	–	–	–	–	Yes	No	No	No	–	Yes
St. Paul's	–	3	–	7	–	–	–	–	–	–	–	–	–	–	–	No	Yes	No	–	–	–
Stafford[11]	2	–	3½	5	–	–	2	–	–	–	2	–	Yes	No	No	Yes	No	No	Yes	–	Yes

½ = Part-time member of staff.

Additional information arising from Questionnaire 1

1 *Barry* *Question 6*

Professional = 2 years
Wing = 3 years

2 *Bedford* *Question 5*

As a women's P.E. college this question does not exactly fit our course requirements. Our work in practical subjects is done in the light of modern knowledge and practice of movement.

3 *Bingley* *Question 6*

Curriculum and subsidiary courses = 2 years
Main course—Movement and Dance = 3 years

4 *Cardiff* *Question 6*

Women: No
Men: Yes

5 *Derby* *Question 3*

All lecturers concern themselves at some time with the teaching of Movement and Dance.

Question 5

(*c*) General course students, men and women, undergo a basic course in Movement. This may be taken by any of the seven lecturers.

6 *James Graham* *Question 5*

(*b*) For Main English students only.

7 *Leeds* *Question 5*

(*b*) Women—a very small part.

(*b*) Men—a very small part.

(*c*) Women—*see* Question 6.

Question 6

Women: No for basic. Yes for main course—extends over two years for the primary and junior secondary students and consists of Movement into expressive work and Movement into skills and agilities.

8 *Neville's Cross* *Question 5*

(*b*) All students take a course in drama—one dance specialist links it with her work in dance.

9 *Ripon* *Question 3*
All do all branches of P.E. with slight specialisation in the aspect they prefer.

10 *St. Mary's* *Question 6*
(*b*) Introductory course.

11 *Stafford* *Question 7*
We acknowledge a fundamental basis on Laban's principles, namely Space, Weight and Time; we do not use his further terminology.

Questionnaire 2

1969

1. Name of college ________________

2. Total number of lecturers in P.E./Movement/Dance — Women ______ Men ______

3. Number of lecturers in Movement/Dance — Women ______ Men ______

4. The number of lecturers in Movement/Dance who have attended the Art of Movement Studio — Women ______ Men ______

5. Do you offer a Movement/Dance course? If YES: — YES NO
   (*a*) as part of a P.E. programme — YES NO
   (*b*) as part of a Drama programme — YES NO
   (*c*) as a course in its own right — YES NO
   (*d*) does the course you offer extend over three years? — YES NO
   (*e*) if a main study in Movement/Dance has been established since 1955 please state year of its foundation ______
   (*f*) if the Movement/Dance course you offer is not included in sections (*a*) to (*c*) but is part of an "induction" course for 1st year students, please state number of hours given to Movement/Dance ______

6. Do you offer Dance as a subsidiary (second teaching) subject? YES NO
   If YES:
   indicate date of commencement of such a course
   within last 5 yrs.
   within last 10 yrs.
   within last 15 yrs.

7. Would you say the Movement course(s) you offer is/are based upon the principles put forward by Rudolf Laban? YES NO

8. Do your staff/students study a method of movement notation? YES NO
   If YES:
   (*a*) as a basic introductory course YES NO
   (*b*) as a continuous course extending over two to three years
   (*c*) as a student's choice study YES NO

9. Do your staff/students study:
   (*a*) Kinetography
   (*b*) Motif Writing
   (*c*) Both

10. If other methods of notation are used please state name(s) ______________

TABLE 4

Question No.	2		3		4		5							6				7	8				9			10
	W	M	W	M	W	M		*a*	*b*	*c*	*d*	*e*	*f*		5 yrs.	within 10 yrs.	15 yrs.			(*a*)	(*b*)	(*c*)	(*a*)	(*b*)	(*c*)	
Anstey	7	2	3	1	2	1	Yes	Yes	No	No	Yes			No				Yes	Yes	No	Yes	Yes		√		No
Avery Hill	10	3	2½	–	2	–	No	Yes			Yes			No				Yes	Y	Ye	Yes			√		No
Barry[1]	5	1	1½	–	1½	–	No	Yes			Yes			No				Yes	Yes	No	Y s				√	No
Bingley[2]	4	3	3	1	–	–	Yes	Yes	Yes	Yes	Yes	Sept. 1966		Yes		√		Yes	Yes		Yes				√	No
Bishop Otter	6	2	–	–	1	1	Yes				Yes							Yes			Yes					
Bretton Hall	2	2	2	2	1	–	Yes			Yes	Yes			Yes		√		Yes	No							
Derby[3]	5	3	2	1	1½	1	Yes	Yes	No	No	Yes			No				Yes	Yes	Yes	No	No		√		
Endsleigh	5	–	3	–	2	–	Yes	Yes	Yes			1966		No				Yes	Yes			Yes		√		
James Graham	½	1	–	1	–	–	Yes			Yes	No			Yes	√			Yes	Yes	Yes			√			
Lady Mabel[4]	10	1	6	–	5	–	Yes	Yes	No	No	Yes			No				Yes	Yes		Yes					
Leeds and Carnegie[5]	3	19	3	1	1	1	Yes	Yes			No			No				Yes	No					√		
I. M. Marsh[6]	16	2	8	1	4	1	Yes	Yes	Yes	Yes	Yes			Yes			√	Yes	Yes	Yes	Yes	No		√		
McMillan	2	1	1	–	–	–	Yes	Yes	No	Yes	No			Yes	√			Yes	No							
Neville's Cross[7]	5	3	2	1	–	1	Yes	Yes			No	1961		Yes				Yes	Yes	Yes			√	√		
North Riding[8]	1½	–	1	–	–	–	Yes	Yes	No	Yes	Yes			No				Yes	No							
Oastler[9]	1	1	–	–	–	–	Yes	Yes	Yes	No	No							Yes	No							
Ripon	2½	–	2½	–	–	–	Yes	Yes	No	No	No			Yes	√			Yes	No							
St. John's[10]	–	8	–	2	–	2	Yes	Yes	Yes	No	Yes			Yes	√			Yes	No							
St. Luke's[11]	–	10	–	1	–	1	Yes	Yes	No	No	No	1958		No				Yes	No							
St. Mary's	6	½	5	–	3	–	Yes	Yes	Yes	No	Yes			No				Yes	Yes	No	Yes	Yes			√	
Trinity and All Saints	2	2	2	–	–	–	Yes	Yes	Yes	No	Yes			No				Yes	Yes	No	Yes	No			√	

½ = Part-time member of staff.

Additional information arising from Questionnaire 2

1 *Barry* *Question 5*
(*f*) Part of professional two-year course for women, *i.e.* one-third of time allotted.

2 *Bingley* *Question 5*
(*f*) In addition to above all students do ten 1½ hour sessions in movement in term 1.

3 *Derby* *Question 10*
In the fourth year only.

4 *Lady Mabel* *Question 9*
Staff study both Kinetography and motif writing, students study motif writing.

5 *Leeds* *Question 8*
But they are introduced to simple motif writing symbols.

6 *I. M. Marsh* *Question 5*
(*c*) In the fourth year B.Ed. course.
Question 8
(*b*) For B.Ed. students only.

7 *Neville's Cross* *Question 5*
(*d*) Whole course at qualifying level is two years.
Question 7
The course in Dance is.

8 *North Riding* *Question 5*
(*f*) Basic course—one hour per week for two years, special course—two hours per week for twelve weeks.

9 *Oastler* *Question 6*
As part of P.E., as a second teaching subject. As part of drama, as a second teaching subject.
Question 7
To a limited extent.

10 *St. John's* *Question 4*
Two attended short courses.

11 *St. Luke's* *Question 5*
(*d*) Over two years.
(*f*) Two hours per week for two terms.
Question 9
The staff study Kinetography and motif writing.

REFERENCE

1. *The Guardian*, 17th February 1970: "Keeping fit—with one eye on the monster," p. 6.

Chapter 11

Conclusion

Man, since he became aware of himself as an entity, has consistently made statements about the world in which he lives and the life he leads. Some acts of expression are beyond words and defy transmutation to canvas, stone or indeed any other medium. The human body alone is a suitable vehicle. From time immemorial rhythmic bodily movement has been recognised as a link between man and the world around him.

The closeness with which the primitives lived to the natural world, their immediate interaction with it and their complete dependence upon things natural very probably gave rise to their consistent use of movement as a means of expression and identification. It is difficult to say whether man attempted to influence his world through movement or influence himself to such a degree that his world took on a less hostile and therefore a more pleasant aspect. Primitive man's movement symbolised or characterised gods, animals or, to him, sublime human qualities and was a central fact of existence. The closeness of his rituals to the ensuing consequences gave purpose and meaning to his movement and helped to give meaning and purpose to his life.

Modern man no longer dances to propitiate nameless gods, bring rain or preserve the fertility of the soil. His intellect and knowledge have carried him beyond this stage and have led him to challenge the environment and attempt to control his existence. Yet these attributes have, in the last fifty years, fragmented, isolated and destroyed the unity of his life. Material needs have been fulfilled by emphasising man's mechanical ability to the detriment of his needs as a human being. On the one hand the inconsequential nature of his work has undermined his pride and often bears little relevance to his leisure, whilst on the other intellectual ability has been elevated to such a degree that the other human qualities and needs have been largely neglected. Many despair of the quality of the life that man has made for himself, the way it has isolated him from his fellows and fragmented the totality of his experience, and constantly search for a means to compensate for these present trends.

Many of the modern methods in therapy return to the fundamental of experience and expression. An acceptance of the power, effect and basic truthfulness of movement enables the disturbed to take the first steps to recovery. In such therapy situations movement is not regarded as a solely physical event but is acknowledged to have other dimensions. The body–mind and mind–body interaction is not doubted nor challenged. Nor is it in the development of the child, where movement enables the child to learn about the world, relate to it and actualise his place in it.

A central theme of the work of Rudolf Laban is the understanding of this body–mind relationship as it is displayed through movement. His analysis of the dynamic content and the spatial form of movement coupled with his method of notation gave him an understanding of man's physical activity which is both comprehensive and detailed. Laban's study of movement, ranging as it did over those aspects of life which produce or require movement, confirmed the interdependence and consistency of the body–mind interaction. Whilst movement understanding is central to Laban's work it does not circumscribe it since movement understanding in itself is a neutral thing. It is the application of this understanding which gives movement study its significance.

The present level of movement awareness in education can be attributed to the way in which dance, drama and physical education have applied Laban's theories and pioneered movement understanding and movement experience. Since his work has been embraced by education it has undergone a simultaneous expansion and contraction. An expansion in as far as the number of people affected by it continues to increase, whilst the scope and opportunity implicit in his work has been reduced because it has only been applied in dance, drama and physical education. The importance of these subjects in the educative process is beyond question, but the movement experience offered by them is only the starting-point of real movement understanding.

Movement is a recurrent and regular feature of education in Britain and we are alone in providing this sort of movement experience as an integral part of a State system of education. This much is well established at grass-roots level, yet there is still a refusal to recognise movement study, divorced from dance, drama or physical education, as a depth study in its own right. Until such recognition is accorded to movement, acknowledging that it is equal in merit to art, science, languages or mathematics, it is impossible for Laban's perspective of movement and the possible development of his work to be accomplished.

Laban's perspective of movement was based on the belief that it is the visible representation of man's personality and inner attitude. He believed that inner attitude could affect movement and movement could influence personality. This reciprocal link underlined the central place of movement in man's life providing him with a means of realising and fulfilling his potential. The analysis of movement which Laban developed provides common reference points for the assessment of individuality and potential as it is displayed through movement; it also provides the means for experiments into the effect of movement on personality.

The practice of movement, as advocated by Laban, is concerned with man's physical and mental activity and is aimed at integrating personality. Laban visualised conscious movement experience as beginning at school and continuing throughout adult life. The dance that has developed from Laban's understanding of movement is a good example of his breadth of vision, for it has opened the possibility of an aesthetic, creative experience to everyone and refuted the belief that such experience is only for the highly talented few. His work in industry, therapy and movement study has not been developed to the same degree as dance and the developments that have been undertaken in these fields indicate that here too Laban's work has enormous potential. Should there be a large-scale development of his work it could add a new dimension to man's working and social life and help to compensate for those pressures which fragment man's existence.

To subscribe to Laban's view of movement is to strive towards an understanding of man as an individual and a member of a group. The depth and scope of Laban's own research is such that he is acknowledged as the pre-eminent investigator into the phenomenon of human movement. His work is recognised as the first systematic study of movement and is the source from which most major movement developments have stemmed and from which still more research can begin. There is now a growing realisation that movement, because it links, conveys and actualises a large part of man's conscious life, is a topic which will require prolonged study. His classification of movement has focused attention upon its important constituents and can give man the opportunity and the means to view his own life in its true perspective. This is possible because Rudolf Laban consistently returns to the belief that movement is the fundamental of experience and expression.

Appendix I

Bibliography

BRUCE V. *Dance and Dance Drama in Education*, Oxford: Pergamon Press, 1965.

CAMERON, W. McD., and PLEASANCE, P. *Education in Movement, School Gymnastics*, Oxford: Basil Blackwell, 1963.

CARROLL, J., and LOFTHOUSE, P. *Creative Dance for Boys*, London: Macdonald & Evans, 1969.

BOARD OF EDUCATION. *Syllabus of Physical Training for Schools*, London: H.M. Stationery Office, 1933.

HUTCHINSON, A. *Labanotation*, London: J. M. Dent & Sons Ltd., 1958 (Reproduction and copyright are held by Theatre Arts Books, 333 Sixth Avenue, New York, N.Y. 10014.)

JORDAN, D. *The Dance as Education*, London: Oxford University Press, 1938. (This book is now out of print.)

LABAN, R., and LAWRENCE, F. C. *Effort*, London: Macdonald & Evans, 1947.

LABAN, R. *Modern Educational Dance*, London: Macdonald & Evans, 1948. Revised edition (1963) by LISA ULLMANN.

LABAN, R. *The Mastery of Mvement on the Stage*, London: Macdonald & Evans, 1950. Reviseod edition (1960) entitled *Mastery of Movement*.

LABAN, R. *Principles of Dance and Movement Notation*, London: Macdonald & Evans, 1956.

LABAN, R. *Choreutics*, London: Macdonald & Evans, 1966.

LAMB, W. *Posture and Gesture*, London: Duckworth, 1965.

LONDON COUNTY COUNCIL. *Syllabus of Physical Training for Boys in Secondary Schools*, London: Inner London Education Authority, 1954.

LONDON COUNTY COUNCIL. *Educational Gymnastics*, London County Council, 1962.

McINTOSH, P. C. *Physical Education in England since 1800*, London: G. Bell & Sons, 1952.

MARSHALL, F. J. C., and MAJOR, E. *A Book of Physical Education Tables*, London: University of London Press, 1940.

MAULDON, E., and LAYSON, J. *Teaching Gymnastics*, London: Macdonald & Evans, 1965.

MAULDON, E., and REDFERN, H. B. *Games Teaching*, London: Macdonald & Evans, 1969.

MINISTRY OF EDUCATION. *Moving and Growing*, London: H.M. Stationery Office, 1952.

MINISTRY OF EDUCATION. *Planning the Programme*, London: H.M. Stationery Office, 1953.

MORISON, R. *Educational Gymnastics*, Liverpool: private publication, 1956.

MORISON, R. *Educational Gymnastics for Secondary Schools*, Liverpool: private publication, 1960.

NORTH, M. *A Simple Guide to Movement Teaching*, London: private publication, 1959.

NORTH, M. *Composing Movement Sequences*, London: private publication, 1961.

PRESTON-DUNLOP, V. *A Handbook for Modern Educational Dance*, London: Macdonald & Evans, 1963.

Readers in Kinetography Laban, London: Macdonald & Evans, 1966–67.

Practical Kinetography Laban, London: Macdonald & Evans, 1969.

RANDALL, M. *Basic Movement*, London: G. Bell & Son, 1961.

RANDALL, M. W. *Modern Ideas on Physical Education*, London: G. Bell & Son, 1952.

RANDALL, M. W. *Modern Ideas on Physical Education*, London: G. Bell & Sons, 1960.

REDFERN, B. *Introducing Laban Art of Movement*, London: Macdonald & Evans, 1965.

RUSSELL, J. *Modern Dance in Education*, London: Macdonald & Evans, 1958.

RUSSELL, J. *Creative Dance in the Primary School*, London: Macdonald & Evans, 1965.

RUSSELL, J. *Creative Dance in the Secondary School*, London: Macdonald & Evans, 1969.

SCHOOLS BROADCASTING COUNCIL FOR THE UNITED KINGDOM. *Facts and Figures*, London: Schools Broadcasting Council, 1969.

WINEARLS, J. *Modern Dance: The Jooss–Leeder Method*, London: Adam & Charles Black, 1958.

Journal of the Physical Education Association, July 1951, November 1951, July 1952, July 1953, November 1953, March 1954, July 1955, March 1956, November 1958, November 1961, July 1967.

Laban Art of Movement Guild Magazine, April 1948, March 1952, March 1954, December 1954, March 1955, October 1955, March 1956, November 1957, November 1958, May 1959.

Appendix II

Personal Impressions of Laban

Introduction

In an attempt to contact people who had been taught by Laban, or had met him, an advertisement was placed in the *Daily Telegraph* during November 1965. A questionnaire was sent to those who replied to this advertisement and the men and women who had worked closely with Laban were approached personally and by letter. It was hoped that by this means a more complete picture of Laban as a man and a teacher would emerge, and that a more exact idea of the impact of his work and the different fields in which it has been applied would be formed.

The material contained in the following pages is a synopsis of the results obtained by these methods. Where a contributor was reluctant to have his name published, I have substituted a number.

Questionnaire replies

Meetings with Laban

The contributors were asked when and where they had met Rudolf Laban.

No. 1 met Laban in 1955 at the Studio. They also met at an Ashridge Summer Course in the mid 1950s.

Ann Garner met Laban in 1947 at the Bradford Civic Theatre School during a two-year theatre course under the direction of Esme Church.

Beatrice Loeb met Laban in 1922, when she was 15, after a performance at Konstanz Theatre, Germany.

Thomas Metcalfe met Laban in 1940 or 1941 at the Bradford Civic Playhouse.

Mrs. P. M. Osmaston met Laban in 1944 at Broughton School, Salford, during her course at Dartford.

No. 2 met Laban in the early 1950s at Dartington Hall, Totnes.

Audrey Wethered met Laban in 1954 during her year's course at the Art of Movement Studio. They also met at courses held at Ashbridge, Y.W.C.A., Studio, etc.,

Miss V. M. Wilson met Laban at a one-man demonstration out-of-doors in the grounds of a boys' school somewhere in Kent. She is unsure of the date. She also met him at a course, called "P.E. problems in the Secondary School," at Reading University, run by the Ministry of Education in 1949 or 1950.

Arthur Wise met Laban in 1948 during a Drama League Summer School at York. He also met him at a Drama League course, "Movement in the Theatre," in about 1949.

Laban as a teacher and a person

Here the contributors stated whether they had taught movement and if Laban's theories were a cornerstone of their teaching. They were questioned on his teaching methods and on how he impressed them as a man.

No. 1 is not and never was a teacher. She was impressed by Laban's maturity and dedication, his humorous insight into himself and others and his deep, mature feeling. He was old and ill when she knew him in 1955, but his maturity was such that she felt a person always gained from his wisdom. He could and did still communicate out of his experience.

Ann Garner did not teach but found Laban's teaching of great value with regard to her work on the stage. His theory for stage behaviour was that there were eight basic movements upon which characters could be built and pupils were given a prolonged exercise with these eight movements in easy flowing sequence. Ann Garner cites as an example that a scatter-brained, jerky sort of person could be based on the "flick" type of movement. "It was amazing how helpful this was as one's voice took on the character of a 'flicking' type of person too."

She was impressed by his energy, his cheeky, twinkling humour and his philosophy that one must never give up. Even if everything one had worked a lifetime to achieve were destroyed one should take a deep breath and start again cheerfully. Laban told her that his life's work had been to collect notes on natural movement based on his own observations and he had been setting down many steps and movements to be used in various ballets. All his manuscripts were destroyed during the war when his house was burned to the ground. He immediately started writing from the beginning again.

With regard to Laban as a teacher, Ann Garner recalls his kind humour and his patience in illustrating or explaining just what he wanted to teach. He had the ability to make each person feel that he was the most important being in the class and that his difficulties and capabilities were of paramount importance. He gave his undivided attention to each pupil and he had the ability to fill each person with a burning enthusiasm for learning and perfecting what he had learnt.

Miss Garner thought it might be of interest to mention that Laban was sometimes asked to visit factories to advise on fatigue in the workers. "I believe it was the Mars Bar factory which he visited and watched the girls packing the bars for some time. He advised that every now and again they should have to lean forward or get up, as their muscles were not having to move enough and were becoming tight and uncomfortable. This of course is time and motion study . . . a thing in which Rudolf Laban was most interested."

Beatrice Loeb, a teacher, wrote that Laban's theories were the corner-stone of her teaching. She found him a wonderful story-teller and was impressed by his understanding, fun, inspiration, kindness, life-long friendship and interest in her work.

Thomas Metcalfe observed that his ideas on the basic nature of movement arising from the elements of time, space and force were the same as Lasker was teaching in connection with the Chess Board. They seemed to him to belong to the first half of this century as those of Stephenson did to the nineteenth.

He was impressed by Laban's belief in his ideas and saw him as a man of the theatre.

Mrs. P. M. Osmaston, a teacher, wrote that it was Laban who first taught us to look at movement scientifically in terms of "time, space and flow." After this teaching all movement could be expressed in these terms.

She found that Laban always seemed rather remote and did not feel she knew him as a man (maybe because he spoke little English). She was impressed by the extraordinary way in which he made the class understand what he wanted from them and the wonderful feeling of elation at the end of his two-hour classes.

No. 2 stated that Laban's theories were a corner-stone provided that a distinction be drawn between dance and physical education using apparatus. She found that Laban's theories have put a different complexion on the teaching of gymnastics, for the stereo-typed "Swedish" has been made more elastic.

No. 2 was impressed by the way discussion of a particular point did go on after the session until the group had reached a satisfactory conclusion. She liked his benign manner and easy mixing with his associates and students and his warmth towards Miss Ullmann and their apparent complete accord.

Audrey Wethered, a teacher, was impressed by his warmth and the way he accepted people exactly as they were; by his humour and geniality, his profundity and yet his simplicity.

She wrote that as a teacher he had an uncanny faculty of knowing how to handle people individually while directing a group, or in a private session. It was amazing what he could get out of people. With wide open eyes he would take in everything and be ready immediately to make use of what he had seen and go on to develop from there. He was able to be with the group, feeling and experiencing with them at the same time as being the observer and leader.

Miss V. M. Wilson, a teacher, was impressed by his dedicated and enthusiastic belief in what he was doing and his ability to involve the class emotionally in achieving the desired results.

She felt uncomfortable in his presence because of his piercing eyes and solid insistent manner and the way he treated the novice as one of a lesser breed and she did not like him.

Arthur Wise wrote that his meeting with Laban changed his views on movement and movement education quite fundamentally. He acknowledges a great debt to Laban's work in his teaching of Speech and Drama. Mr. Wise found that Laban's theories are more of an iceberg than a corner-stone: undoubtedly there but not immediately apparent.

He was impressed by his vigour and the ease with which he established relationships. He said that the man impressed him more than the theory and he remembers Laban's sense of humour which had a touch of pungency about it.

With regard to Laban as a teacher, Arthur Wise stated that Laban was extremely sensitive to the needs of a particular group and had the ability to teach movement as a "total" activity, enhanced by his effective demonstration. Mr. Wise felt that until his meeting with him he had been "drilled" in movement for the theatre as something external to what was going on inside him.

Interviews with those close to Laban

Interview with Sylvia Bodmer

Laban's work was directly opposed to Nazi ideas and was declared against the State (*staatsfeindlich*) by the Nazi government. This was made clear throughout Germany.

Mrs. Bodmer said that harmony of human movement is important but before you can display harmony you must experience disharmony. It is important to experience opposite directions—relaxation, tension, and the same applies in rhythm. She stated that Laban's harmony forms have universality.

She felt that people should not demark Laban's work.

THE MAN

He had vitality and wonderful powers of observation. He was able to bring out latent abilities in everyone. He never gave set exercises and there was no system in his work. He was a man of genius who had understanding plus the ability to develop latent potentials (showing you how you could best develop yourself).

He had a wonderful sense of humour. He was a "deep" type dancer as were Jooss, Wigman and Bodmer.

Laban fought for what he believed in in those early days.

AS A TEACHER

Laban was very vital, dynamic and a hard driver. He expected full participation from his students. He showed terrific intensity because his work was everything to him. He did not pine for an outer show of success. He was an extremely original man.

Interview with Margaret Dunn

PHILOSOPHY OF LIFE

Laban believed that life is movement. He recognised that a person is stronger in certain ways than in others and this reveals his individuality. This applies to races as well as to people. He wanted to help people to strengthen their weaknesses through experiencing their strength and their weaknesses. His movement analysis was very accurate and he maintained that shadow movements reveal the real person.

AIMS OF LIFE

Laban believed that all men should fulfil themselves.

OBJECTIVES

He appeared to have two objectives in Germany—his work in the theatre and his Movement Choirs in which he gave people the opportunity to re-create themselves through movement experience. The movement material for these choirs was taken from life as it was then. This resulted in his being banned from Germany. When he came to England it was in the field of education that he got a start; then he continued his work into industry. Towards the end of his life movement observation and what it revealed was his main interest and then how it could be applied to therapy in order to help patients readjust.

METHODS OF TEACHING

Laban was very constructive, never destructive and could make what was good even better. A teacher must create situations in which the child can develop his own powers. This is what Laban did by giving a movement on which to work (this was the material). In his later years he used people to explore the possibilities of movement.

AS A MAN

Laban was a very acute observer of movement. He could talk with authority on practically any subject—science, psychology—with knowledge. With all his breadth of knowledge he was a very kind man possessing an amazing humanity which put one at one's ease. He always encouraged yet penetrated into the needs of each person—to draw out more than the person thought he had. Laban had deep understanding and perception. He used this penetration to achieve something. He would never say, "You must do this, or to achieve this you must do that." He would never be emphatic on questions which were debatable. He would never give a decision if this would stop people from deciding for themselves. He gave you the ability to think and the experience on which to draw in order to make decisions.

Interview with Diana Jordan

Interest in Laban's work seeped over here from the Continent. During 1926–27 dancers from Central Europe came over to England and visited Bedford College of Physical Education. Later, Joan Goodrich (Mrs. McKnight) was sent over to Europe to study dance with some of the leading teachers, *e.g.* Kreutsberg, and came back to teach dance herself at Bedford College of Physical Education. Miss Jordan met Miss Goodrich, who recommended her to visit the Lesley Burrows Studio in Chelsea.

Lesley Burrows had studied under Mary Wigman, and was already a free-lance dance teacher. She had met and married Leon Goossens. Miss Jordan met her and did three years' training between 1936 and 1938, but before she undertook this training she went to Dresden for the summer of 1935 to study at the Wigman School. While Miss Jordan was studying at Chelsea, Miss Burrows was joined on the staff by Louise Solberg (an American), who had been trained by Laban.

This connection with Solberg led to them immediately being aware of Laban's arrival in Britain in 1938. Burrows, Solberg and Jordan decided to ask Laban to take a summer course in London in 1940. When bombing became very bad in London, Laban moved to Wales and Burrows to Sussex. Meanwhile Goodrich and Jordan were taking courses for the C.C.P.R. The Ling Association was interested in their work and sponsored a Conference at Bushey, inviting Laban, Ullmann, Goodrich and Jordan to teach. This led to the idea of summer vacation courses and through the help of Miss Lloyd-Williams (organiser for physical education in Wales) and her sister, headmistress of Moreton Hall School, both summer and Christmas courses continued until 1961 as "The Modern Dance Holiday Courses," moving as numbers grew from Moreton Hall to Chichester Training College, Dartington, Ashridge to Chelsea College of Physical Education in Eastbourne.

Laban's real interest was people. He once said, "to look at movement is to study people." This led him to study man at work and at play and the need for man to enjoy recreation through dance which he believed would help man to achieve happiness.

Miss Jordan said that we are to study the movement of the human being not movement. Movement aims to increase movement resources and powers of expression and experience in body management. "The carpenter must study wood and its properties before he can use it properly. So with the potter and the surgeon."

THE MAN

Laban was wonderful at drawing out and assessing the individual to find the right way for him. He was larger than life. People tended to stand a little in awe of him, because they realised what a tremendous personality was in front of them. He was tremendously generous, and interested in the humblest of people and creations. Miss Jordan recalled that you left him encouraged and a bigger person. You were less worried about yourself and your own affairs and could look at yourself in relation to others. He was very dignified, had wonderful vitality and a great sense of humour. His classes were electric, for he drew vitality out of people. He had wonderful artistic sense, especially in a dance production, and was a magnificent choreographer, basing his work on his knowledge of relationships in movement.

AS A TEACHER

Laban was not a good speaker and never really mastered English; consequently he found it difficult to put his knowledge into English. As a teacher he was brilliant as there were no problems when he could work practically. He knew best what each class needed and what each lecturer was best at providing.

Interview with Warren Lamb

Warren Lamb first met Laban at a B.D.L. conference in the Lake District and subsequently met him many, many times. Lamb explained that Laban and Lawrence were brought into contact because Lawrence had a niece at the university at Aberystwyth and when Laban gave a lecture there she contacted F. C. Lawrence and told him about Laban. This was how they came to be connected.

Laban worked out methods of movement assessment with Warren Lamb as his guinea pig. Laban was a most intense man with a tremendous personal magnetism. He was a most determined taskmaster with whom there was no letting up. Every minute was used for tutoring and he was a hard driver, both of himself and others. Laban had drive, intensity, power, vision and the ability to bring out the best in everybody. He could see something good in what everyone did. Laban was against any system in his work. ("The element of mysticism in this is unfortunate, for there is great potential in Laban's work in straightforward movement observation and in learning objectively to understand what you see.") Laban was ruthless when driven to it, or when he felt it was necessary.

During the early days of the Studio there were no teachers, only dancers. Lisa Ullmann tried to interest the Ministry of Education and eventually she did obtain recognition for dance. Ministry of Education work has tended to stifle all other aspects of his work.

With beginners Laban taught in stark contrasts. There were much more subtle variations demanded from advanced pupils.

Interview with Geraldine Stephenson

Geraldine Stephenson first met Laban at the Christmas Modern Dance Holiday Course in Sheffield in 1945. She met Laban again when she went to the Studio in Manchester in 1946. In 1948 she became assistant to Laban on work in the theatre.

Geraldine Stephenson remarked upon Laban's dignity, his marvellous sense of humour—he understood the English sense of humour and used this knowledge. He was very tolerant and a great peace-maker. He had a very dominant personality which he could exert at will. Geraldine Stephenson said that he was very still in company and tended to sit and listen. This could frighten until you became acquainted with him. He had a profound ability to see a person's ability and potential—which he exploited and expected others to do the same.

Laban could get the best out of people. He was unpredictable for it was never known what form the lesson was going to take. He never just talked; there was always some movement somewhere. He had drive, determination and conviction in what he was doing. His method of teaching was similar with those who were proficient as with learners. He was a first-class teacher.

He wanted people to learn how to make the best use of their potential and to learn to lead a well-adjusted life. One of his objectives was to learn to understand other people through observation of their movement. People tend to make Laban too complicated. He was always after simplicity.

He became interested in education because the opportunity presented itself. His first love was the theatre.

Laban thought that the writing down of his system might destroy the essence of his teachings.

WHY WAS HE SO DIFFERENT?

He was different because he understood the mind–body–soul combination, and he could translate and put this into motion. He was always exploring, never satisfied with the point that he had reached.

Interview with No. 3
Laban once said to her: "If you saw several of my students dance you would never guess that they had been trained by the same man." This training comprised basic principles of effort, space and shape as set forth in *Modern Educational Dance*. Laban did not like the words: system, method or technique; his was more a way of working. Once having learned these basic principles his students could then use them creatively according to their personality and ability, rather than having to adhere to a set method; thus allowing for endless development stemming from a firm foundation.

Laban was concerned with people as whole beings and aimed to give them a movement experience which was not only what the human body could achieve but was also dynamically expressive, and he used all that they could give individually when working with groups large or small.

In earlier years he worked in dance, choreography, training and observing people's movement in all walks of life; in later years he became particularly interested in the development of personality through movement. Through all this experience he produced and developed his ideas. To mention a few: space harmony, effort qualities, notation for recording both dance and the movement of an individual. From this movement observation he worked out a way of interpretation which enabled him to make an assessment of, and gave him great insight into, a person's true personality. In these observations he found people had movement abilities that were present, latent or lacking. Those that were latent could be developed, but those that were lacking could never be acquired, for the deficiency was due to personality traits.

WHY WAS HE SO GREAT?
Laban had colossal vision. In fact he said to her on one occasion: "There isn't anyone to whom I can really talk." One of his teachers once said to her that he could drop some small remark which she found breath-taking, it was so far beyond the comprehension of the ordinary person, yet opened a door to fresh experience. He made many original contributions to the world of dance and movement in which his achievements were outstanding. Yet when with an individual student, he would give his entire attention and appear keenly interested, as she thinks he was. He had the faculty of seeing a person as she (or he) was, allowing her to be herself and being able to help rather than trying to make her fit a pre-cast mould. By so doing, Laban made it possible for the student to discover certain things within herself. Laban wanted each person to reach the greatest self-understanding of which the individual was

capable and was prepared to drive them if he thought that would help.

He could handle thousands of people in creating dance, bring about relationship between them and produce wonderful art-forms.

Letters on Laban and his work

Department of Education and Science,
Curzon Street, London, W.1.

6th November, 1964.

Dear Mr. Thornton,

Thank you for your letter of 3rd November. Rudolf Laban had been concerned with the application of his ideas to education long before he came to this country and before I met him. He certainly has had a considerable influence on the development of physical education in this country, but the person who could tell you most about him is his close associate, Miss Lisa Ullmann, Art of Movement Studio, Woburn Hill, Addlestone, Surrey. She worked with him before he came over here and continuously in England until his death.

Laban's ideas were certainly contributory to the publications "Moving and Growing" and "Planning the Programme," but many other influences led to the writing and publication of these books.

Yours sincerely,

RUTH FOSTER

17 Holland Park,
London, W.11.

December 2nd, 1964.

Dear Mr. Thornton,

Thank you for your letter and further information. Now that I know more what your particular purpose and interest is I can focus my answers and information along that line.

I am not in the educational field, and my work with Laban has not been in this connection. I have specialised in his movement notation and so from my first meeting with him in 1938 at Dartington Hall, where I attended the Jooss–Leeder School, my association with him has been in connection with the development of the system he originated.

Although my field has been the recording of all forms of dance movement, and theatrical dance in particular, I am aware of how much Laban's basic attitudes toward movement have facilitated this work. The laws of movement which he codified apply to all dance, though many practitioners of the different forms are not aware of this fact. Having departed from his point of view that the elements of movement must be known, recognised, understood and combined as needed for the purpose in hand, the system of notation has been applicable to all forms of movement and the study of this system has proved to be as much an educational process as movement study in other forms.

In the early days Laban devised a personal shorthand to record his space harmonies, this was later developed into another form of writing. Finally he realised that he must have a system based not on his own style of moving but universally applicable. The reason this system, known as Labanotation, or Kinetography Laban, has been so successful rests on the fact that he, as the originator, was so open minded, so conscious of the universality of movement, and that those who subsequently carried on the evolution of the system had also this attitude and point of view as a result of their association with him and/or his work.

Laban could see the detailed and also the thing as a whole. And he was interested in both, and particularly in relationships, how one aspect affected or modified another. Because he made his students aware of the basic truths about movement, the subsequent developments and application of his teaching have not followed the same paths as with a teacher who provides set exercises or ideas. Exploration, investigation, finding out for oneself were part of his training. Not all are capable of taking advantage of this freedom, and many students yearned for material to be dumped in their laps ready made. But this was not his way, and he discouraged in his educational work any establishment of set patterns.

He was a rare man in the wideness of his vision, and in his developing interests in so many fields. In each field he broke new ground by presenting old truths in a new and meaningful way.

As far as his work in the educational field, there are so many here who can evaluate that for you that there is no point in my touching upon it.

You may use my name in connection with the above things I have written.

Trusting this may have been of some help.

Sincerely,

ANN HUTCHINSON GUEST

"Blue Springs,"
Camden Park Road,
Chislehurst, Kent.

Dear Mr. Thornton,

I lived in Kreuzlingen, Switzerland. As a child of 11 years old waiting to become a classic dancer in November 1922 Laban, then

Rudolf von Laban, gave a performance in the nearby town of Konstanz. After the performance I managed to see Mr. Laban who asked me what I wanted. I explained I wished to learn classic dance but that I was an orphan and had no money. Next day Mr. Laban asked me to come to his hotel and was eager to see me dance and move about. He then promised me that I could learn at his school in Rome.

February the following year, I started in Rome my lessons. I had to go and look at paintings and try to move what I had seen; I had to look at buildings and try to move what I had seen; I had to watch people and try to move what I had seen and at the end of it all I danced and created dances myself.

Later on in life I developed movements for suffering people so that they too could learn to dance and be free. I freed children from nervous stress and many a stiff lady in England.

Laban was always thrilled when he could hear what one could do and how one could help through movement. So it went on till he died. An old friend, Father of Movement and Dance, friend of my late husband, my children and all my pupils and friends.

May I add that Laban gave me my studies gratis. Two years ago I gave the Centre a hall so that students can enjoy Laban's theories.

BEATRICE PIA LOEB

9 Ferry End,
Bray, Maidenhead, Berks.

April 5, 1965.

Dear Mr. Thornton,

My first contact with an off-shoot of Laban's work was in 1932 when I met Lesley Burrows (just back from completing her training at the Wigman School, Dresden—with great distinction). Miss Stansfeld, Principal of Bedford College of P.E., gave me a year for extra dance training before joining her staff. With great open-mindedness, she left it to me to select the types of work in which I should specialise—(and the College paid).

I studied with Lesley Burrows and only went to the Wigman School for 2 months in the Summer. Mary Wigman—a pupil of Laban, presented the work very much with her own special emphasis. This centred round the development of the body as an instrument of expression. Exploration of the possibilities was infinite—with no limitations. Beyond that the main headings for training were tension, relaxation, swing, spring, impact and impulse. Dance composition and movement observation were included, but the analysis was not along the lines introduced by Laban into England.

Prior to the gradual acceptance of Laban's work at Bedford all work was formal. Gymnastics were based practically entirely on anatomical foundations and consisted mainly of flexions and extensions and movements isolated to certain muscle groups. All movements were in a single plane. Pendulum swings were considered quite advanced then. All movements were demonstrated and copied.

I cannot remember who was the first to begin applying Laban's principles to the teaching of gymnastics. It seemed so gradual—but certainly one of the people who did most to foster it and prove its value is Miss M. T. Crabbe—principal of the I. M. Marsh College of P.E. She herself did not train in the work but she encouraged her staff to investigate and soon began to appoint people with a background of Laban's work.

I do not agree with your surmise that the fact that men were on active service when the first courses were started, accounts for the more ready acceptance of Laban's principles in Women's P.E. Colleges—but of course you must give your own deductions.

In 1934 (I think) a very large group of men and women P.E. organisers came to Bedford to see a demonstration of the dance (it was called Central European then). The men were most enthusiastic and bombarded me with questions afterwards—but unlike the women—they were not prepared to begin at the beginning and have a go, like the women. In those days Douglas Kennedy used to say that to get the men to take the floor they had to have a drink of cider or beer first! And that was in Folk Dancing.

Lesley Burrows was definitely the first to introduce the work into England. Miss Jordan and I were able to touch a much wider field and so our influence was more apparent.

An interesting point is that when Mr. Laban and Lisa Ullmann first began their courses, they came in for a great deal of criticism because they dwelt so much on twisting, wringing movements. This was their sustained effort to introduce some real flexibility into our vocabulary. Up to then we dealt almost entirely in direct movement.

JOAN GOODRICH

Beechmont Movement Study Centre,
Gracious Lane,
Sevenoaks, Kent

November 27th, 1969.

Dear Mr. Thornton,

My memory of him is of wonderful charm, full of empathy, patience and charity, in the best sense of that word. He was a spell binder, with remote handsomeness, and refinement. His visionary nature was starkly apparent, in his eyes and in his lack of unnecessary movement. Although his work was "action" and its power, he was himself, when I knew him from 1947 to the end of his life, not a man of actions. When I was a young student he appeared, occasionally, to give classes to us. Some of them remain with me as stark experiences I did not understand, and much of the actual movement he asked me to do I did not enjoy, but I remember it. I recall his teaching of the history of dance—where he got his knowledge of it he never divulged and one would not have dreamt of asking. Later I knew him personally and at close range he was quite delightful to be with, rather like the ultimate in understanding fathers. I learnt far more about living from him than I did about movement technicalities. I found that in discussing human issues he talked practically but about movement he talked in principles. My acquaintance with him deepened to a profound fondness and I was very affected personally by his death. But from my second year as a student I was brim full of questions about his theories of movement which were never fully answered. The most usual response to a request for information was on the lines that I was not ready to have the answers. Eventually the "magician" in him overwhelmed my judgment and I came to believe him, and taught in as near a way as I was able to what I understood to be his way. Much as I liked him personally I was uneasy from early on in my training concerning the wisdom of some of his actions. He delegated work to me concerning space harmony, notation and industrial work, years before I was capable of handling them well. This did me a lot of good and I am the richer for it, but his work suffered. I feel that while he was skilful in his education of people, he was almost irresponsible in his handling of his work, particularly with regard to the future of it. I was concerned with several of his publications and was amazed at his choice of material and his handling of it. It seemed to be a real effort for him to come down to earth and to deal practically with his own theories. In part this was due to his poor command of English; in 1947 it was difficult to understand him—while this improved substantially, finer differentiation and style were always a problem for him. But, in the main, his difficulties were factual rather than linguistic. But facts and practical step-by-step building are essential to the translation of a vision into reality. He said many times that it was up to each individual to find the steps for himself, but in practice not many mortals are able to do this well, unless the foundations are laid on rock. And I believe he left the foundation of his work in such a state of liquidity that many of us were bound to founder.

VALERIE PRESTON-DUNLOP